United Methodist

H ANDBOOK

Micheal Selleck

DISCIPLESHIP RESOURCES

P.O. BOX 840 • NASHVILLE, TENNESSEE 37202-0840

www.discipleshipresources.org

Dedication

In remembrance of my mother, Marion L. Selleck,
who personified a spirit of Christian youthfulness

A publication of the
General Board of Discipleship of
The United Methodist Church

Cover and book design by Sharon Anderson

ISBN 0-88177-286-0

Library of Congress Catalog Card No. 99-61200

Scripture quotations, unless otherwise indicated, are from the New Revised
Standard Version of the Bible, copyright © 1989 by the Division of Christian
Education of the National Council of the Churches of Christ in the USA. All rights
reserved. Used by permission.

UNITED METHODIST YOUTH HANDBOOK. Copyright © 1999 Discipleship Resources. All
rights reserved. No part of this book may be reproduced in any form whatsoever,
print or electronic, without written permission, except in the case of brief quotations embodied in critical articles or reviews. For information regarding rights and
permissions, contact Discipleship Resources Editorial Offices, P.O. Box 840,
Nashville, TN 37202-0840; phone 615-340-7068; fax 615-340-1789;
e-mail mgregory@gbod.org.

DR286

Table of Contents

Acknowledgments

Nothing is done in a vacuum, and this book is no exception. A great deal of credit for this volume goes to writers of previous United Methodist Youth handbooks. We all are part of a continuum that strives to show how Christian youth ministry is maintained and preserved for the benefit of sharing the good news of Jesus Christ for all youth, their families, and the local United Methodist churches around the globe.

Specific people shared enormous parts of the load on this project, such as my wife, Chris, whose helpfulness is more valuable and precious to me than I can say; and our children, Amy and Rick, who excused me from more than a few family gatherings while remaining sympathetic.

I am indebted to Terry Carty and thank him for encouraging this opportunity to share my thirty years of ministry in this fashion. Deb Smith, my editor, has been patient and gentle throughout this process, and she is much appreciated.

Others have also supported me during the writing: Mac Brantley, Bettye Corcoran, Pam Higgins, Winnie Hoover, Jeni Lee, Tim McDaniel, Bradley and Emily McEntyre, Mozelle Mitchell, and Derrick Rhodes. These folks covered many bases for me, and I genuinely appreciate their steady and gracious support.

The names of other family, youth workers, former youth, church folks, mentors, and friends are legion and are all part of many years of thoughtful reflection, corrective instruction, Christian charity, and grace. Many of these people are the same ones who touch your lives in various ways. If ever a book was born out of our collective experiences, this may be it.

My prayer is that the hand of God has been and remains in the midst of this work and the work that all of us perform as a response to God's hand upon our hearts and heads. To God be the glory.

Mike Selleck

Foreword

This is the UNITED METHODIST YOUTH HANDBOOK. As the word *hand-book* indicates, this is a basic reference that provides a solid foundation for ministry by, with, and for youth. It is a guide that gives the reader operating instructions for developing and implementing youth ministry that will help make disciples of Jesus Christ.

Mike Selleck has drawn from his vast knowledge and years of experience in youth ministry to create a handbook that will become a standard guide for pastors, Christian educators, and congregational leaders of youth ministry. This book is filled with proven wisdom for creating and sustaining a vital youth ministry.

Use this book as your foundation. Seek out additional books, resources, and people to help you build on the foundation provided by this resource.

One of the limitations of a book is that it contains a fixed number of pages that cannot be changed once the book is in print. This can result in a resource that quickly becomes outdated. We are excited that this hand-book combines the convenience of an easy-to-use basic manual with a continually updated on-line appendix. Within this book you will find basic information that does not change substantially over time. In the on-line appendix (**http://www.gbod.org/youth/UMY_appendix.html**) you will find cutting-edge information related to the newest developments in youth ministry. Think of the appendix as an idea bank where you can make deposits and withdrawals. You can read about the ideas others have had to improve their ministries with youth, and you can share your own ideas. The interactive nature of the appendix creates exciting new opportunities for youth leaders to communicate with one another, to gain critical knowledge, and to respond quickly to the emerging needs of youth.

Youth Ministries Staff
General Board of Discipleship of The United Methodist Church

Using This Resource

This youth ministry handbook is written for United Methodist youth and adults. This is your handbook. The intent is to help leaders, in response to God's guidance, discover a vision for ministry with youth. It is also meant to be a practical guide to help plan and implement effective youth ministry in local congregations.

If you are new to youth ministry, you may want to begin by reading the whole book, highlighting sections that relate to your situation. As you gain experience, you will want to refer back to particular sections as specific needs and questions arise.

Balanced Christian youth ministry offers participants significant ways of living out Christian discipleship. As you read this book, keep the word *balance* in mind. Each teen who enters into the ministries of your church is unique and is at a different place in his or her faith journey. What helps one youth may not do much for another. As youth grow, physically and spiritually, they benefit from a variety of methods and approaches.

Achieving balance in youth ministry doesn't happen quickly. It is a long-term endeavor. While you are trying to discover and to maintain a healthy perspective in your ministry, make it a habit to follow in the way you intend to lead:

1. Maintain a diligent, daily prayer life.
2. Smile deeply.
3. Surround yourself with individuals who can help you discern if you are asking the right questions and seeking Godly answers.
4. Laugh graciously and often.
5. Keep your own devotional life vital and alive.

This handbook is full of suggestions, ideas, recommendations, and possibilities. Nothing, however, should be construed as more important than the response Jesus gave to the Pharisees when asked which commandment was the greatest: " 'You shall love the Lord your God with all your heart, and with all your soul, and with all your mind.' This is the greatest and first commandment. And a second is like it: 'You shall love your neighbor as yourself' " (Matthew 22:34-39). All ministry, with youth or with others, is rooted in the timeless truth of beginning and ending all we do with God's commandment. Lead in love, for God and for others.

Chapter

So What Is Youth Ministry?

The Church's Mission

The General Conference of The United Methodist Church is the only body that can speak for the entire church. In 1996 it stated that the mission of The United Methodist Church is to make disciples of Jesus Christ. This simple statement is the guiding principle for all ministry, including ministry with youth. We are in ministry with youth to help youth and those who work with youth to be faithful disciples of Jesus Christ.

Youth Ministry All Week Long

Not too many years ago youth ministry was often a single weekly time slot geared to providing wholesome group activities for teens. This included Sunday night programs, hayrides, camping trips, relay races, scavenger hunts, skits, and so forth, all designed to keep youth engaged and connected to the church.

Today much has changed. Youth ministry is no longer viewed as a once-a-week occasion with a single group of teens. Instead, church calendars offer a variety of times, locations, and themes for different youth all week long, such as:

- Sunday morning study classes and contemporary worship.
- Sunday afternoon youth choirs and leadership planning.
- Sunday evening youth gatherings.
- Late-night faith-sharing circles.
- Monday morning prayer breakfasts.
- Tuesday evening Bible studies.

- Wednesday drama rehearsals and tutoring opportunities.
- Thursday after-school huddles.
- Friday sunrise prayer clubs.
- Saturday service projects, and many more opportunities on a once-a-month basis.

While there is a time and a place for hayrides, bowling, and other forms of relaxation, balanced youth ministry must offer opportunities that go well beyond fun and fellowship. Teens today want more than icebreakers and pizza snacks. They need and seek Christian opportunities, not idle time fillers.

A Youth Ministry Inventory

Youth ministry is everything that includes, affects, invites, or touches the lives of youth within your congregation. Chances are your church already offers a much fuller range of opportunities for youth than most youth are aware of. Use the following list as a starting point to identify the scope of your youth ministry. As you seek to establish a balanced and healthy youth ministry, begin with the items you have checked and grow from there.

Youth participate in the worship life of the congregation as:
- ❑ Ushers
- ❑ Acolytes (candle lighters)
- ❑ Liturgists (Scripture readers)
- ❑ Greeters
- ❑ Leaders of a youth Sunday service
- ❑ Leaders of Easter sunrise service
- ❑ Musicians
    - ❑ vocal choir
    - ❑ bell choir
    - ❑ playing instruments
- ❑ Members of dance or drama ministries
- ❑ _____ (list others)

Youth have opportunities for fellowship through:
- ❑ Youth group meetings
- ❑ Church picnics

❑ Church sports teams
❑ District and conference activities
❑ _____ (*list others*)

Youth provide leadership through:
❑ Serving on church boards or committees
❑ Working with vacation Bible school
❑ Working as an assistant in the nursery
❑ Serving as an officer in a church-based group
❑ Participating in lay outreach or evangelism programs
❑ Serving as a delegate to annual conference
❑ Participating in district, conference, and national opportunities
❑ Teaching a Sunday school class
❑ Leading a Bible study
❑ _____ (*list others*)

Youth learning opportunities include:
❑ Bible study
❑ Sunday school
❑ Share/care groups
❑ Special short-term study groups
❑ _____ (*list others*)

Youth service opportunities include:
❑ Mission trip
❑ Christmas and/or Thanksgiving projects
❑ Visits to healthcare centers
❑ Outreach programs to the community
❑ Christmas caroling
❑ _____ (*list others*)

The Purpose of Youth Ministry

Each autumn, churches gather their youth together with a few adults and try to decide what to do. As common as this may be, its approach is a bit backwards. It's far more appropriate to first determine the purpose of having a youth ministry and then to organize in a simple way to live out that purpose. So what is the purpose of a United Methodist youth ministry? Consider the following:

Christian Foundation

Youth ministry should provide experiences and opportunities that teens probably would not have with other groups. If churches simply duplicate programs of other groups aimed at young people, why exist? Recreation is a great tool for establishing relationships; but if games are the sole focus of a youth ministry, youth will go other places that meet their deeper needs. This is why worship, study, outreach, and service receive emphasis alongside fellowship in a balanced approach.

Growth in Faith

One of the greatest gifts church youth ministry offers is a safe space where youth can explore who they are and who God is calling them to be. Youth today are bombarded with demands and messages telling them who they should be. An effective youth ministry is a place where young people can find support to put aside the competing voices in order to hear and to respond to the voice of God. Your youth ministry may be the only place a young person has to experience such safety.

Help for Daily Life

An effective United Methodist youth ministry provides opportunities for youth to examine their experiences and values as they intersect with real-life issues. Your ministry can provide occasions for youth to ask, "Why am I here?" "What happens to me when I die?" "What is my relationship with the people I live with?" and "What difference does it make how I live my life?" These kinds of questions can be the focus of youth group discussions and Bible studies.

Leadership Development

Youth ministry should provide for development of youth leadership. In youth ministry, the focus is on giving youth opportunities to lead. Your youth ministry may be the only group in which a particular youth will ever have the opportunity to be a leader, developing self-esteem as he or she learns and practices leadership skills.

Healthy Relationships

An effective youth ministry is invitational; that is, it is easy to enter. Offer youth a place where they feel welcome. Let them become part of a core of youth who support each other through times of feeling lonely, misunderstood, or rejected. Every human being needs to have a place where he or she is accepted.

The five purposes explained above help youth grow toward becoming disciples, or "learners"—not having all the answers, yet choosing to follow the Christian life. You will discover that your faith will grow as you journey with others.

What Is Our Task?

"There shall be a comprehensive approach to development and implementation of youth ministry programming at all levels of the Church. The comprehensive approach is based on the understanding of the primary task of youth ministry: to love youth where they are, to encourage them in developing their relationship to God, to provide them with opportunities for nurture and growth, and to challenge them to respond to God's call to serve in their communities." (From *The Book of Discipline of The United Methodist Church—1996.* Copyright © 1996 by The United Methodist Publishing House. ¶1118.2, page 480. Used by permission.)

Let's look a little further at the four elements of the primary task of youth ministry.

Love Youth Where They Are

Accept the youth as they come. See them first as they are, not as you think they should be. The Christian love in your heart should be the first thing a youth notices about you and should be a constant component in all your ministry. Teens choose to become part of a youth ministry for many reasons. Some may attend for social amusements or mission projects, because another particular youth is there, or just to get out of the house. All these reasons are acceptable, and a youth should be welcomed regardless of the reason.

Encourage Them in Developing Their Relationship to God

Be intentionally Christian in focus. The expectation of a life of discipleship and commitment to Christ should be a steady hum throughout all the fun, laughter, study, prayer, travel, worship, service, special events, and discussions.

Provide Them With Opportunities for Nurture and Growth

Establish a variety of ministry opportunities that take seriously their levels of understanding and commitment. Each youth is typically at a different place on his or her faith journey.

Challenge Them to Respond to God's Call to Serve in Their Communities

Create opportunities where youth can plan, lead, and participate in service ministries. These can take place in the church, the schools, the community, anywhere they go! Give youth a chance to understand how and why the good news of Christ is spread throughout the land.

To say it another way, The United Methodist Church envisions youth flourishing in the world as faithful disciples, beginning right now. It can happen! And you, the leader of youth ministries, can help it happen.

The Whole Church's Ministry

"But God has so arranged the body, giving the greater honor to the inferior member, that there may be no dissension within the body, but the members may have the same care for one another. If one member suffers, all suffer together with it; if one member is honored, all rejoice together with it." (1 Corinthians 12:24b-26)

It is a mistake to view youth ministry as separate from the rest of the church. The Scripture from Corinthians reminds us that all the ministries of the church are connected. When youth ministry becomes separated from the ministry of the congregation, the youth and the congregation suffer. Effective youth ministry requires the support, encouragement, and accountability that comes from being part of the church family.

A Vision for Youth Ministry

We have already stated that the mission of The United Methodist Church is to make disciples of Jesus Christ. A vision guides how you will live out this mission within your church. While the mission provides the frame or the boundaries for your youth ministry, the vision is the picture of what you are striving for your youth ministry to be. If you were to paint a picture illustrating God's intentions for youth ministry in your church, what would it look like? How would this picture compare to the picture for the entire congregation?

Developing a vision or "picture" is an important step in any ministry. When we are all looking at the same picture, it is easier to determine what we need to do to make our reality look like the picture. A vision leads us into an intentional future.

You will have created a workable vision statement when everyone can agree on and state clearly the vision of the ministry. Once these statements are written and understood, planning decisions come more easily, and effectiveness is more accurately measured. Ministry is designed with an intent that is in harmony with the other groups in the church. In other words, youth ministry is purpose-driven rather than pastime-driven.

Consider the following steps when developing a vision statement:

1. Ask all members of the congregation (including youth) to pray and search the Scriptures for guidance in clarifying what God is calling the congregation to do and to be.

2. Design a listening event or events where youth and adults can be heard. Record what is said during the events. Ask these questions:
   - Why do youth from our church want to get together?
   - What is the purpose of our youth ministry?
   - What do we want youth to gain from being a part of our youth ministry?
   - What is God calling us to be in this day and place?
   - Who are the youth with whom God is calling us to be in ministry?

3. Form a team that includes youth and adults to process the results of the listening events and to formulate a vision statement.

4. Test the statement with youth and adults.

Having struggled with what God is asking your youth ministry to be, you will be better equipped to plan for ministry that will move toward the vision.

Leaders bear the responsibility for guiding everyone toward the vision and for holding everyone to the vision. Both youth and adult leaders are committed to living out the vision when:

- They are enthusiastic about their roles.
- They listen carefully and regularly.
- They are willing to think and plan flexibly.
- They are dedicated to constant and continual improvement.
- They are challenged by the prospect of change and growth.

Who Is Included in Youth Ministry?

"The term *youth ministry* is an inclusive title, encompassing all the concerns of the Church and all activities by, with, and for youth. The youth ministry of The United Methodist Church shall include all persons from approximately twelve through eighteen years of age (generally persons in the seventh grade through the twelfth grade, taking into account the grouping of youth in the public schools), who are currently or potentially associated with the church or any of its activities. Youth who are full members of the church have all rights and responsibilities of church membership except voting on matters prohibited by state law." (From *The Book of Discipline of The United Methodist Church— 1996.* Copyright © 1996 by The United Methodist Publishing House; ¶258.2, page 149. Used by permission.)

Following is a brief explanation of some of the above terms:

All Activities by Youth

This includes anything that youth lead. We should encourage this level of activity all the time.

All Activities With Youth

This includes anything that youth and adults do together and should include the bulk of youth ministry activity in a local church.

All Activities for Youth

This includes anything that adults do for the benefit of youth (essentially without youth input or assistance). This element has its place, but should be the smallest category of the three listed here.

All Persons From Approximately Twelve Through Eighteen

The ages are listed because not all youth are in school and yet those youth are still in need of the loving, saving grace of Jesus Christ.

Generally Persons in the Seventh Grade Through the Twelfth Grade

Some youth programs reach out to younger people to prepare them to enter into mainstream youth ministries in the near future. Some churches offer opportunities to individuals beyond the formal age to reinforce their faith walks as they enter young adulthood. The way that youth are grouped in schools may affect how churches decide what ages will be considered as youth. For example, in a community where sixth graders are part of a middle school, the church may want to include sixth graders in the youth ministry.

Youth Currently or Potentially Associated With the Church or Any of Its Activities

The church youth ministry includes youth in your community as well as those in your congregation. Participation in a United Methodist youth group does not require youth to be a member of your church.

What Is a Youth Coordinator?

"The coordinator of youth ministries and the youth council, when organized, shall be responsible for recommending to the church council activities, program emphases, and settings for youth. The coordinator and council shall use available resources and means to inform youth concerning the Youth Service Fund and shall cultivate its support: *provided* that prior to this cultivation or as a part of it, the youth shall have been challenged to assume their financial responsibilities in connection with the total program and budget of the local church." (From *The Book of Discipline of The United Methodist Church—1996.* Copyright © 1996 by The United Methodist Publishing House; ¶258.2a, page 149. Used by permission.)

The congregation looks to the youth coordinator for direction in matters of its youth ministry. Seen as the lay person who holds the "big picture," the youth coordinator promotes the development of a comprehensive youth ministry. The following suggestions will help youth coordinators carry out their ministry:

- Maintain a prayerful perspective of the entire youth ministry of the church.
- Become acquainted with as many of the youth as possible.
- Become acquainted with each of the leaders, teachers, and officers of youth.
- Become educated on the nature of adolescents, their needs, joys, and concerns.
- Work with others to identify the particular needs, abilities, and desire of the youth.
- Be aware of youth participation in all church activities.
- Serve as an advocate of youth involvement in church planning and decision-making. (Encourage the appointment of at least two youth to each local church committee, council, and so forth.)
- Serve as a primary assistant to adult volunteers working with the youth, including seeking resources, budget support, and solutions to other needs that volunteers have to accomplish the church's vision for youth ministry.
- Attend the meetings of the church council and youth council (or similar bodies) in your church. Call attention to overlapping dates

and other concerns. Keep before the council the need to be sensitive to the ability of youth to participate in and to profit from the activities being planned.

- Talk with your pastor about his or her concerns and suggestions for youth ministry. (The pastor should be a primary source of information about youth ministry opportunities in your district, conference, and jurisdiction.)
- Work with each teacher and leader of youth (small membership churches) and/or with the youth council (larger membership churches) to plan and to evaluate youth ministries.
- Make recommendations to the church council concerning leadership training needs of workers with youth.
- Meet and plan with each ministry team chairperson (missions, worship, evangelism, education, stewardship, and so forth) to discover what the ministry team is planning for youth and to suggest emphases needed by youth in that area.
- Be alert for announcements of training events for age-level and family coordinators, youth coordinators, adults who work with youth, and youth who lead.
- Have a conversation with the district and/or conference coordinator of youth ministries. (Consult your pastor for the names of these people.)

For More Help

The Book of Discipline of The United Methodist Church—1996. Published by The United Methodist Publishing House. Available through Cokesbury (800-672-1789).

Guiding Youth Ministries: 1997-2000. Available through Cokesbury (800-672-1789).

Youth in Charge: How to Develop Youth Leadership (SkillAbilities for Youth Ministry), by Tami Bradshaw and Jeff Huber. Published by Abingdon Press. Available through Cokesbury (800-672-1789).

Chapter

2

Where Do We Start?

Help! I'm a New Youth Coordinator

The first-time youth coordinator can easily be overwhelmed by the seeming enormity of the task. So what are the most important things on the list? What goes first? Use the checklist below to organize your initial tasks:

- Pray for guidance. Invite God's closeness as you embark on this new, exciting ministry. Ask God to give you a mind open to learning, a heart ready for loving, and hands receptive to working.
- Talk to other adult workers with youth. Discuss the tasks of the youth coordinator with adults who have worked extensively with youth. Your search may take you to other local churches. Spend time talking with the parents of your youth; they have much wisdom to share.
- Talk with the pastor and other church staff. Ask your pastor, Christian educator, church musician, or other staff members whose work involves youth to share their experiences, insights, resources, and suggestions. They can lead you to helpful printed resources.
- Talk with youth. This step should not be overlooked: Ask the youth of your congregation (those who are active and those who are not) to tell you about themselves—their struggles, hopes, dreams, fears, and daily lives. This conversation will take time to develop; many youth believe that adults do not want to listen to them honestly. Be patient. As youth discover your willingness to be open, receptive, and caring, they will share more of their life narratives.

- Develop a team of adult workers with youth. Call an initial meeting of all adults interested in learning more about working with youth. Pray, study Scripture, share experiences, and develop a sense of community. Begin planning an approach to youth ministry at your church.

Developing a Youth Ministry

- Review the major themes in this handbook. Discover what the major issues are today and what directions things are moving in. Don't rely on what was happening in the denomination ten years ago or even five years ago. Make some phone calls and talk to those responsible for youth ministry at the conference and denominational level. What are the current strengths and weaknesses? Why have some things worked and others failed? What is on the horizon?

- Decide what purpose God may have for your church's youth ministry. This is an important consideration, and the issue should be discussed in all circles in the church. When you know why something is being done, it is much easier to plan and implement it.

- Survey the families in the church and community. Try to pinpoint their needs and interests. Inquire about time pressures and limitations. Knowing the parameters of the families eases planning.

- Develop a vision for youth ministry. Ask yourself: *What should the range of this ministry be? What should the intent of this ministry be? What should the leadership of this ministry be like? How will this ministry be perpetuated?*

- Determine what the youth need. What sort of organization do age, maturity, community activities, school involvement, and so forth dictate for our teens?

- Know the skill level of your leadership. What training is needed? How can that training be provided? Are there people who aren't involved but should be? Where will young people themselves be able to provide leadership?

- Determine how extensive a youth ministry the church can support. Are there enough people in your church who are willing and able to support all the programs you have in mind? Realize that the amount of support available for your youth ministry will not be greater than what the church is able to provide.

After you've given these issues prayerful consideration, move forward with the input and involvement of many other people—the ones who will be in service and who will be served by this ministry.

Starting New, Starting Over

The following suggestions may help you think through some critical considerations as you develop a new youth ministry or as you redesign an existing ministry.

Identify a Team of Listeners

Identify youth and adults willing to become a team for the purpose of working through this development or redevelopment process. This should be an objective and committed lot. If your church is small in numbers, and you have less than eight youth, perhaps everyone should participate. If you have a larger church, and getting everyone together is difficult to coordinate, select a team from a good cross section of youth and adults.

Listen

Talk with the church members, boards and committees, youth, parents, pastor, other youth leaders in the community, police agencies, social service agencies, and your own district and conference youth leaders. Try to discern what people are thinking, expecting, needing, and hoping for. This data gathering, while tedious at times, provides valuable information.

For those who have existing programs, there is some history sharing that needs to happen. Interview older youth who have memories of days gone by: Find out what worked, what didn't, and why. If there were events where things went woefully wrong or wonderfully right, try to learn about them, including what can be gleaned from those kinds of times.

Have an In-depth Bible Study

After the data is compiled and shared, and the team has a good handle on the facts, go to the Bible. Begin to look at what God is calling you to be and to do in light of the data you have gathered.

Share Your Findings

If you have done the proper kinds of fact-finding with your congregation and community, there will be some people eager to know how things are going. Don't keep your process a secret. (It's a model that the other ministries in the church might like to emulate.) Ask for time during official board meetings to make a report. Let the youth do the reporting. Adults should strive to be in supporting roles, not in directing ones. Reporting to the church keeps the congregation involved and informed. Good ideas, additional adult support, funding, and goodwill come out of a well-presented report.

Begin Implementation

Begin to implement those aspects of your findings that are appropriate, supported by the church and pastor, and fit with the overall direction of your vision.

A word of advice: One of the deadliest approaches to starting or reviving a youth ministry is to begin by asking, out of the blue, "Say, gang, what do you want to do?" This approach is nonproductive for several reasons.

- Youth typically have little experience with envisioning what a new group might do or could become.
- A group gathered for the first time has not had the opportunity to wrestle with identity questions that need to precede programming decisions.
- Trying to get off the ground with broad questions tends to make people feel uneasy. When people are new to the concept of a ministry and/or to each other, such questioning usually creates more self-consciousness than it does enthusiasm.

Plan the First Three Months

When beginning or revitalizing a ministry, begin a habit that will serve you well for many years: Develop and plan a three-month block of detailed ministries.

- Take the time to physically create a calendar of events and opportunities, weekly youth meetings (if that is your choice), midweek events, retreats, or whatever your fact-finding, Bible study, and sharing process suggested.
- Identify fellowship time, theme speakers or leaders, recreation, worship, and service opportunities.
- Assign responsibilities, including who will do what and by when.
- Identify how you will promote this first three months. Some suggestions: Inform and use your pastor, church bulletin, church

newsletter, and community newspaper. Display posters around your church building. Send a handwritten invitation to each person on your contact list and follow up with phone calls or visits. Ask for time so that youth can present their plans during Sunday morning worship, in addition to asking the pastor to make announcements from the pulpit.

Organization can't be stressed enough, and ministries that are healthy and balanced always have this at their core. Three months of detailed planning should always be in front of you, regardless of the time of year. Some larger groups plan as far as two years ahead for major activities and six to eight months for weekly activities. When this level of organization exists, last-minute flexibility and responding to God's movement is done more easily.

This level of organization isn't to preempt the prayerful and discerning work that should go on immediately prior to and during these events. However, God is able to guide our energies and paths three months ahead as well as three hours ahead. The key is taking the time and practicing the habits to allow God a hand in the process from beginning to end.

What will be different this first time is that only the small team of youth working on this project will have input as to what the first three months will be. After that, the process must be opened up so that others will have a hand in what is being planned and done.

The Leader's Assignment: A Parable

Two leaders stood on a riverbank studying a turbulent white-water, eager to take on the challenge in their canoes. The first leader, after discussing with her youth, explained to her group they could shoot the rapids, but first they would empty their canoes and carry all the food and gear down below the rapids. The youth could then take turns spotting each boat as it maneuvered its way through the treacherous waters; that is, they would stand on nearby boulders with ropes in the event of a capsizing. After a bit of time and work, the youth were in position. One by one, each canoe was watched as the occupants successfully and safely negotiated the churning water.

The second leader, having navigated many similar rapids with no trouble, was confident her youth could manage the passage without the delay of hauling gear and taking turns standing on rocks. The leader explained that when everyone was ready, one by one the canoes should shoot for the middle and paddle like the dickens. The first one bounced through upright. The second, heavily laden, spun sideways and became perilously pinned against a rock, blocking the path for the third canoe. The crashing of the boats was barely audible above the roar of annoyed screaming paddlers. The last canoe capsized, dumping its passengers and that day's evening meal into the river. The second team scurried about, fishing youth, canoes, and gear out of the river below the rapid. A while later, the leader and youth were safely ashore. They were a bit tired, still wet, and pondering what they could salvage for an evening meal.

Which leader showed true leadership? If you answered, "The one that anticipated the possibility of trouble and took the time to keep her team safe through the passage," you are correct. But what she showed wasn't water safety; it was the highest quality of Christian leadership: love.

The greatest quality of a Christian leader is love, and it is basic to guiding and working in youth ministry. When you lead from a life that reflects and projects love, you bear witness to the heart of God, and you open souls to God's possibilities in ways nothing else can.

A Measure of Success

People who spend a lot of time doing youth ministry talk about "what works." They are usually searching for or telling someone else about programs that were successful for them. Yet what works in one case may not work in another.

There are several ways to measure success. Some consider a ministry to be successful if it made the youth happy. Others measure the number of youth in attendance. Today there seems to be a shift in defining "what works." The move is away from measuring the number of participants and toward measuring the involvement of individuals in discipleship practices and disciplines that result in transformed lives. Some use a bit of both.

In youth ministry, an emphasis on following Jesus (discipleship) provides youth with a model of being in the world in an understandable and transformational way. Discipleship is based on identifiable practices and disciplines that can be learned, enhanced, and redemptive in daily living. Youth ministries that focus on discipleship help youth face life and make sense of their daily experiences.

For More Help

For youth ministry questions, write the Director of Youth Ministries at the General Board of Discipleship, P.O. Box 840, Nashville, TN 37202 (phone, 877-899-2780; e-mail, umyouth@gbod.org; website, **www.gbod.org/youth**).

For events and resources in your area, contact the people in your district and on your annual conference staff who have responsibility for youth work. Your pastor can give you the names and phone numbers.

LifeGivers: A Practical Guide for Reaching Youth in a Challenging World. Published by Abingdon Press. Available through Cokesbury (800-672-1789).

Chapter

3

Why Have a Youth Council?

The Benefits of Having a Youth Council

A youth council is a way to share and teach responsibility and to increase involvement and relevance. Adult leaders may find it more expedient to do things without a youth council, but in the long run, a youth council will lead to a ministry by and with youth, rather than a ministry for youth.

A council on youth ministry strengthens youth ministry by:

- Involving others.
- Partnering youth with adults.
- Keeping the entire youth ministry in focus: study, service, fellowship, the arts, worship, outreach, sports, administration, and so forth.
- Developing youth leadership.
- Giving youth a voice in decisions.
- Providing a forum for new ideas.

What Does a Youth Council Do?

A youth council's tasks are fluid, reflecting the times, needs, and understandings of the church. The following list is an overview of responsibilities:

- Evaluates the scope of youth ministry, making recommendations so that present and future needs of youth are addressed.
- Coordinates and schedules all youth events.
- Keeps the other youth informed.
- Reports to the church council (or equivalent body).
- Provides a forum for churchwide information that youth need.

- Works with the congregation's nominations and personnel committee to recommend youth members to other official groups. (Remember that youth may serve on all boards and committees except as trustees—the law requires trustees to be adults.)

The Adult Role in a Youth Council

Youth leaders, instead of adult leaders, should be allowed to carry out the bulk of the duties. Initially this may not be an easy thing to do. If a council is new, it will take time for the youth to understand what is expected and to be able to fulfill the expectations. While they learn these things, be gentle with them. Support them in their successes; walk with them in their failures. In all cases ask this question with love, "What did you learn in this experience?" Let them answer for themselves. If adults quickly begin rescuing youth from the consequences of their actions or non-actions, little significant learning takes place. A youth council is an important way for youth to discover and to develop leadership abilities.

A well-functioning youth council takes extra time, greater attention to detail, advanced planning, and a commitment to follow through. In short, it takes organization. It is better not to have a youth council than to have one in which adults make all the decisions.

Does a Small Church Need a Youth Council?

A benefit of smaller groups is ease of inclusion and movement. If you have few numbers, you may call together all youth and adult leaders to review ministries under the church youth umbrella once or twice each year. Procedures can be kept flexible. Responsibilities can be rotated and shared with ease. Coordination of youth events can be comfortably shared. Consider these steps:

- Meet with all youth and adults for a review of the big picture of youth ministry in the congregation.
- Establish a worship atmosphere and spend time inviting the presence of the Holy Spirit to the planning.
- Review or develop a vision statement: What is the purpose for having a youth ministry? Why are we doing this planning? What do we need to accomplish?
- Plan the annual calendar of responsibilities, ministry opportunities, and special events.

- Assign responsibilities for planning and follow-up.
- Establish when the next meeting will be.
- Acknowledge and celebrate God's hand in the work.
- Dismiss with prayer.

What About Larger Churches?

Larger and more diverse youth ministries may choose to develop a more formal youth council to assure all parts of youth ministry are cared for. Consider these steps:

- Establish regular meeting times, monthly or quarterly.
- Determine who should serve on the council.
- Hold an annual planning retreat for the leadership. At this event the youth ministry vision statement is reviewed, affirmed, and embraced; the calendar is established; and assignments are made. Different general task areas such as missions, music, and worship can be set up. Or specific task groups can be established, such as the spring retreat task force, the mission trip task force, and the youth Sunday task force. A blend of both is typical.

Who Serves on a Youth Council?

Membership on the council preferably should include at least two youth for every adult. Youth members may include:

- One or two representatives from Sunday school classes.
- One or two representatives from the junior high and the senior high youth group.
- A representative from each other youth ministry group (youth choir, Youth DISCIPLE Bible Study, Youth Covenant Discipleship Groups, and so forth).
- A few at-large members. These may be filled by youth from your church who are involved at the district, conference, jurisdictional, or national level.

Adult members should include as many of the following as possible, while keeping the ratio of two youth for each adult:

- Coordinator of youth ministry.
- Sunday school teacher.
- UMY adult leader.
- Representative from other church youth ministries.

- Representative from the church council or equivalent body.
- Parent.
- The pastor and/or the employed youth worker.

Selecting Youth for the Youth Council and Making Other Decisions

It is important that every individual who wants to be involved in leadership has the opportunity to do so. How are individuals selected to participate in the leadership positions of a youth council? How are decisions made in the youth council? Review the following possibilities and select the model that works best for your situation.

Voting

Any process involving elections needs to be handled carefully and thoughtfully, or you can easily end up with people elected for the wrong reasons. It is possible to have teens elected to positions because of popularity, rather than because of their abilities to lead effectively in a particular position. In any election there are winners and losers. For many teens losing an election can be damaging to self-esteem. Be careful if you use this method.

Voting works well for issues that need to be decided quickly, or when everyone's support is not necessary to implement the plan. For example, voting may be the most effective way to decide if you will have pizza or hot dogs at a youth event, but it may not be an effective way to decide if the youth will commit to serving on a regular basis at a homeless shelter.

Discernment

Discernment puts decisions into a faith perspective before choices are made. Discernment brings focus to issues using a specifically Christian light. Taking time to quietly consider the council of the Holy Spirit inspires those involved to make wise and faithful responses. Discernment requires a certain level of faith maturity and an atmosphere of worship and prayer. It is a more faith-filled way to make decisions.

For discernment decision-making:

- Choose and maintain an attitude of worship.
- Meet in a worship setting.
- Open with centering songs or liturgies.
- Read relevant Scripture that calls for wisdom and maturity.

- Offer prayers for the same.
- Present the issues, one issue at a time. (Maintain a worshipful atmosphere.)
- Encourage questions of exploration or clarification.
- Distill the dialogue into a focused single question.
- Call for a five- or ten-minute time of silence for Godly reflection.
- Ask for insights gained. If there is no consensus, try once more.
- Seek creative responses to God's leading by blending or reshaping ideas until a sense of having met God's intent is reached.

The discernment model is particularly appropriate when dealing with important issues that need the support of the entire group.

Invitation

Another model of establishing a leadership team is by invitation. There are two types:

- **Individually**

Calling people individually by name is the way Christ selected his disciples. Inviting people by name suggests several things: You know them; you recognize gifts in them; and you respect their ability to do something or to be effective in some meaningful way. This method requires a skilled leader who can see potential and who can help develop those God-given gifts, however latent they may be. Strive to find meaningful work for every youth who seeks an opportunity.

- **Collectively**

In this method, announce a meeting time and place for all those interested in leadership. Those who show up constitute your youth council. From there you can help them discern task groups for various areas or events, choose officers (if helpful), and more. Different groups may take on specific tasks such as the annual winter retreat, the summer high adventure trip, weekly devotions, monthly mission projects, or the Christmas pageant. It may be that the group senses God leading them to work on these as a team.

Sign-Up

Create a sign-up board with descriptions of each office or team available. Invite people interested in serving in a leadership capacity or on a committee to sign up during a specific period of time. If a list contains only one name, that person is automatically placed in charge. If several people sign up, members can meet together and discern their own leadership.

Planning a Youth Council Meeting

The following guidelines will assist youth who are serving as leaders.

Before the meeting:

1. Work with adult members to prepare an agenda, and have it available to hand out or to post on newsprint.
2. Clear all arrangements for a meeting place.
3. Gather resources that will help in the group's work (calendars, curriculum materials, *UMY Handbook*, lists, and so forth).
4. Send reminder notices to those who are to attend.

On the meeting day:

1. Check the meeting place for comfort and a good work setting, preferably chairs around a table.
2. See that necessary supplies are on hand, such as newsprint, marker, tape or tacks, and program materials.
3. Post the agenda.

During the meeting:

1. Use the prepared agenda to guide the meeting.
2. Everyone in the leadership group has responsibility for keeping the work moving. Any member should be ready to ask:
   - Is the topic clearly defined (or the issue adequately explained) so we can understand what we're dealing with?
   - Do we have all the necessary facts before the group?
   - Have we had enough time to examine the facts?
   - Can we postpone action, or does some decision have to be made now?
   - What possible solutions are we considering?
   - What decisions have we reached on these matters?
   - Who has been assigned what responsibilities?
   - How can we speed up this process?
   - What questions must we answer before we can proceed to a decision?
   - How do we plan to evaluate the results of this decision?

3. If the meeting seems to be bogged down, check for difficulties:
   - Are the goals clear?
   - Are too few persons doing all the talking?
   - Is there an unwillingness to work at the task?
   - Are personal feelings getting in the way?
   - Are there not enough facts?
   - Are the issues confused and confusing?
   - Is someone dominating?
   - Are we getting off the subject?
   - Is there a clear sense of direction?

Once difficulties have been identified, redirect the discussion, clarify issues, summarize previous discussion, and ask questions to get the meeting back on track.

4. Encourage follow-through by:
   - Assigning responsibilities.
   - Making specific appointments.
   - Setting preparation deadlines.
   - Clarifying how something is to be done.

5. Set times to check on progress.

6. Remember to say, "Thanks for a job well done."

7. Be ready for emergencies. The unexpected will happen. All of us "goof up" at times.

8. Evaluate what was done and how it was accomplished. What do we want to remember for next time?

Chapter

The Web of Discipleship

Gateway Ministries

Stand-Alone Ministries

Ongoing Ministries

Outreach Ministries

Teach, Reach & Receive Ministries

Inviting Youth

Professing Youth

Committed Youth

Curious Youth

Cautious Youth

There are only three directions people can travel on the web in relation to the center, which is Christ. They can move toward or away, or they can circle. Many of us spend the bulk of our faith journey circling. Personal growth or faith crisis may find us suddenly moving in or away, only to then circle again until the next personal change.

Reaching Out to Cautious Youth

Before ministry with youth can begin, there needs to be an audience. Begin by reaching out to the youth around you: the church, area schools, sports complexes, fine arts programs, stores, and clubs. These are the youth God has placed in your view. These are the ones you should be introducing to the good news of Jesus Christ. How this introduction takes place is important because many youth today are suspicious of the church and the message they don't understand.

Begin with an attitude check. Remove the lenses of expectation about what is acceptable, normal, average, and relevant for today's youth. Holding out acceptance of certain youth until they conform to some preconceived Christian ideal is a misrepresentation of God's grace. It's like waiting until a teenager is no longer hungry before letting him or her have dinner.

Characteristics of Cautious Youth

It's vital to understand that many youth outside the church are uncomfortable and unfamiliar with the church and what it's about. They are cautious about visiting or letting their defenses down in unfamiliar territory. Carefully plan ministry at this level in non-threatening and nonjudgmental ways. Activities and even the language used should be chosen thoughtfully. The priority with cautious youth should be taking time to know them as individuals and showing them, rather than telling them, the love and acceptance of Christ.

Gateway Ministries

Ministries at this level are gateways for people to jump on the web of discipleship. The intent is to allow cautious youth to meet other people of faith, youth and adult, and let them know, more by actions than by words, that they are welcome as they are. Keep activities temperate, festive, and yet entirely purposeful. Keep prayers short and rooted in the experiences of the youth. Don't put cautious teens on the spot in front of other youth with hard or personally revealing questions.

Ministries to Consider

Fellowship events or programs that happen away from the church building can include movies, miniature golf, cookouts, team sports, day trips, concerts, amusement parks, pizza parties, and fundraising events.

Things to Remember

- Greet the youth individually by name.
- Learn something about them—likes, interests, gifts, or talents they have.
- Seek to know them as God has sent them, looking for goodness and potential.
- Find ways to need them; ask them to help you with things.
- Expect them to come again. Anticipate them, and celebrate when they do.
- There's an old saying that people don't care what you know until they know that you care. This is particularly true for cautious youth.

When they trust you care about them, they will, on their own, begin asking about doing things together that indicate they are moving to a different place on the discipleship web.

Ministry With Curious Youth

Youth today are as hungry and as curious for spiritual meaning as any generation of people has ever been. Youth circling at this level on the web aren't totally convinced that the Christian life is for them, but they continue to attend because they enjoy the people and the ministries. They know the songs, the prayers, the leaders, and what is expected; but a personal relationship with Jesus Christ still doesn't make sense to them.

Characteristics of Curious Youth

Youth at this level are coasting through your ministry opportunities. This is another way of saying they haven't engaged themselves in anything that is specifically meaningful for them. They may be waiting for the right kind of opportunity, the right kind of invitation, or the right kind of mentor. Whatever it may be, your task with the curious youth is to stay close until you can get a sense of what it is that piques their interest. It may be helping with planning, serving in a mission, working with a tutoring program, reading Scripture, or just about anything that will engage them in meaningful work.

Stand-Alone Ministries

These are good kids with good hearts and good intentions. They deserve our best efforts at keeping them engaged and involved until they make the move to a different place on the web. When a match between their curiosity and meaningful work is made, they may be ready to progress. Focus on relating them to other Christian youth and adults; plan for and anticipate them. Plan for short-term ministries of less than four meetings or components. If longer commitments are required, they tend to find ways to coast around it rather than to become engaged.

Ministries to Consider

Guided service opportunities and brief studies can include beginning Bible study; singing for convalescent homes; working in mission work camps; collecting items for Thanksgiving and Christmas baskets; serving at a soup kitchen; taking part in brief studies on the Ten Commandments, the Beatitudes, global concerns, or an overview of the Old or New Testament; or watching a movie with discussion following.

Things to Remember

- Let your life, language, behavior, choices, and habits be a visual witness for how an individual relates to God.
- These youth are more open to what they see, rather than what they hear. Share basic biblical ideas and Christian concepts. This doesn't mean pushing them to make decisions. First let them see these notions in practice in your life and in the lives of other adults and youth they look up to or respect.
- Invite them to participate with others; significant relationships with a few other youth and an adult is a priority.
- Look for teaching moments to nudge them into thinking about ministry opportunities at a deeper level.

When they find a vehicle or interest that piques their curiosity, they may be willing to follow it to a new place on the web.

Ministry With Committed Youth

When youth reach this place on the web, what you offer in terms of ministry classes or events is less important to them than simply being with the group. Where you will be is where they will be. They like you; they like the programs; they attend whatever happens next and anticipate whatever you're offering. These are the youth you count on as regulars for just about anything you are planning.

Where we make a mistake with this group is when we equate their regular attendance with a personal relationship with Jesus Christ. In fact, many teens at this level are still not convinced of this truth for their own lives. They simply like being with the group and doing the things you do.

Characteristics of Committed Youth

These are typically good, honest, upright, and in many cases very moral and considerate teens. They just haven't made a choice for themselves yet to accept Jesus Christ as their personal Savior.

Ongoing Ministries

Ministry at this level should focus on opportunities for a decision for Christ. Don't be one-dimensional with commitment evangelism; there are many ways to come to Christ and many ways to make a decision. If we offer only the way we experienced salvation for ourselves, we are cloning, not evangelizing. Paul was blinded during a trip; Jacob wrestled all night with an angel; and John the Baptist was filled with the Holy Spirit even before he was born! Get the picture? God is creative and quite capable of reaching us in many ways, and we should be as versatile as we can be to prepare others to receive God's salvation.

Ministries to Consider

Ministries to these youth include service opportunities to the congregation and community and longer-term studies such as helping with vacation Bible school; ushering or greeting for Sunday service; running audiovisual equipment; serving at church dinners; tutoring; hosting parties or picnics for children's homes or hospitals; helping with a city recreation program; joining a Covenant Discipleship Group; studying other religions and denominations; and taking part in weekly Bible study groups, retreats, and sermon discussion groups.

Things to Remember

- Invite them to participate in the full life of the church through study, worship, and service offering a grounded lifelong journey of faith.
- Demonstrate and talk about Christian values.
- Provide opportunities for nurture and growth in Christian faith and daily life.

- Establish the Bible as the primary guide for Christians. Do this through studies, discussions, devotions, and reflections. Keep a Bible visible; use it and know it.
- Establish prayers as a key discipline for Christians. Study prayer, practice prayer, and model this for youth.
- Invite youth to commit their lives to Christ. When they are presented with the right challenge at the right time, they will accept the call to commit their lives to Christ and to move to the next level.

Ministry With Professing Youth

At this place on the web, youth have made a commitment to have Jesus Christ at the center of their lives. At this level youth will want to learn how to be better followers of Christ, and they will want to know what to do to reinforce this life choice. The kinds of opportunities you offer at this level need to reflect this growing interest in deeper spirituality and discipleship.

Characteristics of Professing Youth

It's common to see youth at this level turn their backs on those who have not made a conscious decision for Christ, even the ones in their own youth ministry. Often it begins with complaining that programs aren't religious enough, which is also a way of saying other youth are not as important as we are. Eventually they stop attending events designed for cautious and curious youth altogether, because it's "a waste of their time." Paul teaches in Romans 12:3-13 and again in 1 Corinthians 12:4-27 that we are all part of the Body of Christ, and until this is behaved as well as believed, we're not as close to God as we may think.

Outreach Ministries

Ministry at this level should focus on a deeper faith walk (developing Christian habits, using the means of grace) and on living as the Body of Christ. It is also at this level that you can begin to encourage youth to lead in discipleship activities, teach, and take part in other ministry roles.

Ministries to Consider

Opportunities include taking part in worship, helping with ministry to the congregation, and having a freer hand in outreach to the community. Youth might serve on appropriate church committees; help with new member visitation; write a column in the church newsletter or bulletin; design and lead a worship service for children; take part in a clown ministry; write prayers or litanies for use in worship services; pray at congregational functions; witness personally in worship; help with children's sermons or puppet shows for children; and prepare short messages for a local radio station.

Things to Remember

- Go slowly and don't take it personally when it seems as if they are not growing deep enough fast enough. A deep faith is something that is grown in one's spirit, not acquired in a single lump.
- Help youth practice expressing their faith in a variety of ways: writing, movement, words, art, liturgy, voice, and actions.
- Help youth understand that what others see them doing is as instructive as what others hear them saying.

When teens on this place on the web understand that we are all incomplete as long as any one part of us (another person) is not on this web of discipleship; when they realize that it takes different kinds of outreach to reach different kinds of people; when they begin to see cautious, curious, and committed youth as persons they can effectively reach, then they open up and begin to move to the next level on the web.

Ministry With Inviting Youth

These are deeply committed Christians who know and appreciate the differences in teens. They willingly give up their own agendas to do whatever it takes to get others onto the web of discipleship, and then they walk with them as they circle and grow toward Christ.

Characteristics of Inviting Youth

Youth at this level know you don't get others onto the web by just sending them invitations and telling them where the group meets. They don't say things like, "See ya there!" Real inviters know that a genuine invitation means telling cautious youth what time they'll pick them up; taking them to the place where the group meets; and staying with them from beginning to end. Inviting youth understand that without a constant flow of new youth on the web, the day could come when there are no youth on the web at all.

Teach, Reach, and Receive Ministries

Ministry at this level should focus on shared strategies for reaching new youth, leadership training under other qualified teachers, and opportunities for significant leadership in the larger church.

Ministries to Consider

Ministries can include participating as a leader and a guide—leading many of the ministries already listed, such as mentoring other youth; coaching a team, either sports or spiritual; or leading a short-term Bible study.

Things to Remember

- Encourage youth to keep up a vital prayer and devotional life, including daily Bible reading.
- Provide an accountability group for spiritual direction, nurture, and clarification. (See Covenant Discipleship Groups on page 115.)
- Without significant and meaningful responsibility, youth may feel they are not necessary and may slip away.

Balance on the Web

Knowing your potential audience and what keeps them engaged helps you visualize and create a balanced youth ministry with a clear direction everyone can understand and work with.

As you review the present ministries you offer youth within the total scope of your church (See the inventory list in Chapter One.), determine whether each opportunity appeals more to the cautious, curious, committed, professing, or inviting type of youth. Then place a dot for each opportunity on the appropriate spot on the web. After you've placed all your opportunities on the web, look for balance.

If there are too many dots on the outer rings, you may not be allowing youth enough opportunity to grow spiritually as they make a commitment to Christ. If you have most of your dots in the inner rings, you may not have adequate ways for new youth to join your ministry. Balance means having at least one dot on each ring before you have two on any ring. This means that there is at least one non-threatening, fun, gateway program to reach and to receive new youth; another opportunity available when they're ready to grow into something a bit more challenging;

another dot for those who like being with the others in longer commit-ments; a deep Christian-based faith opportunity for those who have given their life to Christ; and a place to keep inviting youth involved in reaching out to others.

Numbers Decrease as Commitment Increases

We know that most youth today are not on the web at all; they are not involved with the church at any level. We can assume that the next largest segment of youth is the cautious group, followed by the smaller curious ones, followed by the still-shrinking number of committed kids, and even fewer professing and inviting youth.

When ministries are developed primarily for professing youth, we are targeting a rather small segment of youth and are not providing for the largest segment of teens just beginning their Christian journey. Balance means taking each level of youth seriously and prayerfully. If your planning is alienating more youth than are being invited, how faithful to the Great Commission are you? Instead of asking only, "Who is here?", ask "Who is not here?" What segments of youth are not repre-sented? Why? What needs to happen to continue to reach and to receive new youth, keep them growing in their faith walk, and allow them significant opportunity to be meaningfully involved in the life of future ministries? These kinds of questions and subsequent answers will help you create a balanced and effective ministry.

Note that it is difficult to have a "once-and-for-all" balanced youth ministry design. Ministry changes constantly with the changing needs of the youth. If a church has a youth ministry that is the same each year without dropping or adding anything, then it will probably begin to lose impact with the youth and will eventually lose participation.

Know Your Youth

The World Your Youth Live In

Just as there are no universal youth, there is no universal youth culture. If you want to know more about the world your youth live in, a bit of poking around will be necessary. Working through the following steps may be helpful as you sort out the particular culture of the youth you are serving or the youth you would like to reach.

Create an Age/Grade Timeline

Draw a single line and break it into segments that match the ages or grades of the youth you are working with: lowest on the left, highest on the right. On that line, place a mark for any and all major events your youth typically deal with, such as entering high school, getting a driver's license, and attending prom. Knowing what major changes and rites of passage your teens typically go and grow through will help you understand when they may need support and guidance. These also may be times when they are particularly open to suggestions and instruction.

Create a Weekly/Daily Timeline

Examine what goes on in a typical week of a teen in your area. If most ride a school bus, that's a good beginning point. If they have a strong soccer program with endless weekend tournaments, that's a consideration, as are all sports, athletics, fine arts, and any other components. When do they have free time, and where do they spend it? Review school times, eating times, family times, and recreation times. Your ministry must take place within the environment of their daily lives. It's difficult to plan ministry and reach real people when you cannot foresee the rhythms of their weekly lives.

Review Family Matters

Families do matter! The impact families make, positively and negatively, in and on the lives of teens is well worth noting. Knowing more about the youths' families allows prayers and plans to be more specific and informed. Some things to know about each youth include:

- Who is in the immediate family?
- How many parents live in the household?
- What is the religious background of the family?
- Is the family a blended family?
- Are the parents supportive of the youth's involvement in church activities?

Review Media Influences

Youth today are bombarded by media of every type. What media most affect the teens you are concerned with? What magazines or books are they reading? What radio stations, cassette tapes, or compact discs are they listening to? What television shows are they watching, and what media do they discuss when they get together? Do they chat about daytime television or Internet sites? How do they connect with each other? Are they linked to each other by telephone, by e-mail, or by driving back and forth to each other's houses?

Review the Pressure Points

What forces shape and push at the lives and goals of teens in your area? Most youth experience a good deal of stress around the issue of grades on their schoolwork. This may be parental pressure, but it also may reflect a deeper concern about their future, such as qualifying for college, choosing a college, deciding on a career, and pondering what will be their overall effectiveness as an independent adult.

Review What Youth Revere

Some youth think the world begins and ends with sports; others focus on cars, jobs, parties, or friends. The list can include anything that is important to the youth in your area. It is important to realize that many youth value what is handed on to them by the traditions and attitudes of the community. Regardless of how or why, at least know what the areas of reverence are. For negative influences, these deeply rooted forces are to be reckoned tactfully, using grace and patience. Head-on attacks usually put people in a defensive posture and could end up reinforcing their positions, rather than causing them to think things through.

Review Their Heroes

Knowing who youth admire, venerate, and want to be like are all important things of which to be aware. Some follow their "guru" with outward and visible signs such as what they wear, how they act, and what they pay money for. Others are more subtle, showing few outward signs. Reaching teens who admire sports legends would be handled differently than reaching teens who look up to musicians. Even which musicians are being admired is important to know, as you may approach those who look up to a rock-and-roll singer differently than those who revere writers of Broadway music.

Review Your Alertness Aptitude

This may sound arduous, but give it consideration. Gather the adults in your church who work with the youth. Review the names of each youth in your ministry, one by one, asking this question, "Who in this room is alert for this teen?" This would mean noticing each teen's attendance or lack of it, lifting him or her up in prayer, perhaps making a phone call from time to time when appropriate. (Please note: This isn't authorization to shadow or fawn over a teen, nor should this be viewed as authority to counsel or to serve as a surrogate spiritual guide. This is merely a way of making sure that each youth has someone who is maintaining an awareness of that youth so that he or she doesn't fall through the cracks.)

Walking through these components should help you and others in youth ministry to be sensitive to the world in which your youth live their daily lives.

Nurturing the Whole Person

In seeking to minister to the whole person, strive to address these traditional domains: physical, spiritual, intellectual, emotional, and social. Here is a quick inventory:

- Physical: recreation, nourishment, haven, safety, and so forth.
- Spiritual: worship, prayer, time with God, stillness, and so forth.
- Intellectual: Bible study, training, discussion, exploration, and so forth.
- Emotional: honor, significance, belonging, respect, and so forth.
- Social: fun, friends, liveliness, play, mentors, and so forth.

How Do Youth Learn?

I have always loved crossword puzzles, so when I needed to come up with a creative Advent program, I knew just what to do. I was certain my youth would get excited about a big wall-sized crossword puzzle to be filled in with Advent and Christmas words. I spent hours creating clever clues with reasonable answers to acquaint my youth with the meaning of the season.

As the youth trickled into the youth room that night, I thought I was with a herd of groaning cows. I discovered almost none of my youth liked doing crosswords. That hour, one of the longest in my ministry, taught me that when youth have no interest, nothing is interesting.

Most people ask how to teach youth. I wish more folks asked how youth learn. It is a critical distinction. The first question focuses on what is going on with the leader, and too often planning stops there. For example, since I like crossword puzzles, I assumed my youth would like them; or if I had felt like being serious, I might have assumed everyone would enjoy a serious and deep program. The emphasis is on the wrong person—the teacher. The more appropriate approach is to begin with the hearer—the learner.

While focusing on the youth and the learning rather than on the adults and the teaching is the best way to start, it is only the beginning. Several issues come into play when we look into the learning process and what it means for youth ministry.

First, make sure you know what your goal for the session is. Knowing what you want the hearers to learn is critical to a successful encounter. What do you want to get across? Where do you want to end up?

Second, how can this idea be best communicated with your particular group? Think about the people in your group. Then think about possible methods of getting across the main idea. Decide which method(s) best communicates the goal.

People have specific ways they learn best. To maximize learning, vary teaching methods. One program might use music heavily; another might emphasize service work; and still another may stress debate and discussion. Better still, learning how to blend several techniques into the same session will communicate to a greater variety of youth.

Life Issues

Adolescence is a normal phase of life. Each youth will follow his or her own inner time schedule in the transition between childhood and young adulthood. Listed below are some of the developmental issues with which youth are dealing.

Developing Meaningful Relationships

Relationships are important to adolescents. In their efforts to be accepted, junior high or middle school students in particular dress, talk, act, and believe the way "everyone else" does within their circle of friends. It is important to model acceptance and openness. Youth need to feel free to talk about their friendships. Adult leaders can help youth mix and mingle with group members by using deliberate icebreakers and by designing small-group tasks.

Younger teens search for a sense of identity within groups. Older youth begin to differentiate themselves from groups and to establish their own identity. Significant adult relationships provide role models for moral values, understanding, and behavior. Adolescents who do not have adult mentors may model themselves after peers that perpetuate immature, irrational, and unthinking behavior.

Dealing With Sexual Feelings

Early adolescents have an awakening of sexual feelings. Television, movies, music, and advertising bombard them with messages about sexuality, often causing increased confusion. Ministry with youth and their parents should include sex education from the Christian perspective. With increasing numbers of adolescents engaging in sexual activity and with the high risks associated with sexual activity, it is imperative that teens be presented with a Christian understanding of sexuality.

Developing Self-Esteem

Youth are inwardly focused (how they look and how they think they look to others). They are aware of their differences in maturation and are sensitive to feelings concerning self-image that influence their self-worth. Include games, relational activities, and topics that promote cooperation and affirmation, rather than the all-familiar competition and putdowns present elsewhere in our society. Leaders also should be sensitive to games and activities that are difficult for the overweight or otherwise challenged youth.

Teens struggle to understand and to know what their feelings mean. They struggle to control their feelings in a socially acceptable way. Help youth deal with stress, depression, and tension in their lives by using patience, by providing positive activities (singing, games/community building, and service to others), by loving them, and by accepting them.

Racism is a reality for many ethnic youths. It can have a negative impact upon their outlook on life, self-concept, and self-esteem. All youth work to discover "who they are." For ethnic youth in particular it may be important to claim and affirm their ethnic heritage. Be sensitive to the unique experiences of ethnic and cultural groups. All cultural groups bring richness to the larger culture and should be treated with dignity and respect.

Developing Personal Ethics and Moral Values

Adolescents are developing critical thinking, decision-making, and problem-solving skills. Newly able to think about their future and the kind of society in which they want to live, they begin to struggle with abstract principles and ideals such as liberty, justice, and love. Parents and adult workers with youths often get the full-force dosage of adolescent unlimited and untested "think" power. They are passionate with unbridled idealism about the world. Provide a safe place for youth to express their visions, and provide opportunities for youth to act on their beliefs. Help intellectual growth by providing interesting and challenging experiences where youth can learn firsthand about limits. This in turn helps prepare them to make better choices.

As young adolescents begin to think abstractly, they are able to imagine what others are thinking about them. This leads to the peer group becoming increasingly important and authoritative. Personal conflicts arise when the church differs from the peer group. Youth usually will go along with the peer group at this point. Be informed enough to talk about conflicting moral issues when the opportunities arise. Provide "safe zones" (nonjudgmental, non-threatening) where honest, genuine discussions dealing with moral issues can occur. Direct youth to Scriptures for help. Provide a listening ear and loving direction while being willing to let them struggle for their own answers. Young people must be allowed the opportunity to change their minds about previously stated opinions. Teach empathy and compassion for and about each other. It's important to find ways to affirm, listen, love, and care for them.

Our faith connects with everything we do—each struggle and each success. A nurturing church provides a sense of safety and support as individuals grow in their faith. Caring adults—Sunday school teachers and other adult workers with youth—offer timely experiences and activities that encourage decision-making, guide youth through developmental transitions, and always make sure they are aware of God's love and care for them.

Youth With Disabilities

Youth ministry is meant to be inclusive—all youth feeling safe, accepted, included, and loved. We must strive to create environments that emphasize unity and community, highlight the wonder and awe of diversity, and yet discover the wonder of oneness in Christ. Youth with physical or other types of disabilities may need particular help to fully participate in the youth ministry of your congregation. These disabilities may include things such as attention deficit disorder, autism, dyslexia, learning disabilities, hearing impairment, visual impairment, and restricted movement.

Learn as much as you can about the types of disabilities found in the youth you work with. Teachers, parents, and the youth themselves can provide suggestions of what will make the youth ministry more accessible for the youth with disabilities.

It is important to understand disabilities and to work at being both accessible and inclusive. Crucial to this whole process, however, must be affirmation and unconditional love and acceptance. The variety of our abilities and our limitations is a mark of God's fingerprint on our individuality. In all your plans, all your language, and all your work at hospitality, highlight the deeper fundamental knowledge that God is a God of grace and has given us talents, gifts, and insights to share.

Differences Among Youth

We must guard against easy generalizations about youth. Young people are individuals with unique combinations of interests, abilities, needs, backgrounds, experiences, doubts, and dreams. Helping youth affirm their unique identities is a crucial part of being in ministry with them.

Be sensitive to differences that are products of ethnic and cultural diversity. These areas reflect different experiences that, when appreciated and understood, can greatly enrich shared group life. Prayerfully monitor your sensitivity to avoid being influenced by patronizing attitudes, self-righteous behavior, or veiled hostility.

Different interest orientations are always present in a group. Different interests can be related to school activities, attendance at different schools, hobbies, skills, varying degrees of ability, and different family backgrounds. Many of these differences should be celebrated in their own right and have potential strengths to build on in the group.

For More Help

The Search Institute is committed to practical research benefiting children and youth. Their website is **www.search-institute.org**.

The National Middle School Association is an organization for those interested in the educational and developmental needs of young adolescents. Their website is **www.nmsa.org**.

Chapter

6

What About the Bible?

The Bible and Youth Ministry

As Christians we are people of a specific book: the Bible. As Christians we believe that the Bible reveals a living God whom we know in Jesus Christ. We believe Jesus Christ is the living Word of God, and to know the living Word of God, we must know the Bible.

Scripture lies at the heart of United Methodist youth ministry. This sacred book confronts us with what it means to be God's people; provides guidelines for living responsibly in our world community; and is the essential resource for whatever we do through the church. Biblical understanding through study is the lifelong journey all Christians are on.

The Bible includes many different types of writings: poetry, letters, laws, histories, wisdom sayings, and more. While the Bible is a diverse book, it has a unity because of the story it tells. The Old Testament tells the story of the encounter between God and the Hebrew people in the events of their history. The New Testament is based on the life and teachings of Jesus Christ, the new covenant between the people and God. It includes a history of the early Christian church as it became the vehicle for spreading the news that all people could have a relationship with God.

Use the Bible in your youth ministry. This book is too important to be left on the shelf when planning discussions, worship, and reflection times after service projects and fellowship activities. Too often in youth ministry we think that the Bible belongs mainly in Sunday school and is not necessary in the other aspects of youth ministry. Don't make this mistake! Through Bible study, you will be offering a resource to youth that they will not be able to get in any other group to which they belong.

Why So Many Kinds of Bibles?

The original texts of what we know as the Old Testament were written in Hebrew, while the New Testament was written in Greek. However, there are no existing original copies of these manuscripts. For example, we do not have the original letters that Paul wrote. In their place are thousands of slightly different manuscript fragments. These were written at different times, reflecting changes in use of language, each suggesting a reasonable, yet different, way of reading the Scriptures. This makes an accurate single translation problematic. After extensive research and careful study, a number of Hebrew, Aramaic, and Greek translations have been accepted by the scholastic community. These form the basis for the Bibles we read today, and they come in three categories.

Verbal Translations

Scholars who translate ancient texts into word-for-word modern languages (or as close to it as possible) create what are called verbal translations. These texts are more concerned about translating the words themselves, rather than trying to convey what the words meant in the context and culture of the day in which they were written. Common versions that fit the verbal translation category are the King James Version, the New International Version, and the New Revised Standard Version.

Interpretations Based on Early Ancient Texts (Dynamic Translations)

People wanted a Bible that non-Christians could understand with only a small degree of sacrifice of word-for-word accuracy. This meant a Bible that was still based on the ancient languages but translated into the everyday vernacular of regular people. Bibles in this grouping include the *Good News Bible: The Bible in Today's English Version* and the more recent *Contemporary English Version.*

Interpretations Based on Other Modern Bibles (Paraphrase Translations)

These versions aren't based on those scholarly Greek, Aramaic, or Hebrew translations. This group of Bibles attempts to make a current translation even more readable and understandable by paraphrasing the Bible into everyday street language. Notable Bibles from this category are *The Living Bible* and *The Message: The New Testament in Contemporary English.* Since paraphrase Bibles don't maintain a link to the Greek, Aramaic, or Hebrew translations, they cannot, nor were they designed to, support serious Bible study.

Suggestions for Using the Bible With Youth

Offer a variety of Bible classes regularly, not just in short bursts or for special liturgical seasons. You have different kinds of youth, and they will require a variety of approaches as their spiritual and intellectual needs change and mature. The following suggestions represent a spectrum of possibilities that could be a regular part of your ongoing youth ministry.

Get the Pastor Involved

Seek a time and a place for the pastor to actively teach the Bible to the youth—for instance, a specific weekend retreat, a six-week course, or any focused setting that puts the pastor in the role of Bible teacher with the youth.

Offer a Variety of Times

Organize Bible classes for different days during the month or week, and for different time slots: mornings, evenings, and after school. Also stagger the length of the classes, offering some that are short (even as little as half an hour), some much longer, and some in between.

Offer a Variety of Approaches

Structure opportunities to approach the Bible from different angles: Some groups might be grounded in factual investigation, while others might be based in sharing reflections and insights. And another might be based on looking at Scripture that relates to specific issues in the lives of teens.

Encourage and Model Personal Bible Study

Don't let the demands of youth ministry lead to neglecting the need for your own regular personal Bible study. It's difficult to inspire youth to make Bible study a life habit if it isn't true for their leaders.

How Do I Lead a Bible Study?

Bible studies can be done in dozens of different ways. Here are some examples.

Read Through the Bible in One Year

This is a good way to get acquainted with the whole scope of the Bible. Getting a feeling for the whole Bible can make focusing on one section or one type of literature at a later time more relevant. There are several programs that offer guided reading programs for 365 days.

Focus on Old Testament and/or New Testament Overviews

This is similar to reading the Bible from beginning to end, but usually takes less time and focuses on the big themes rather than on reading word for word. This is a good place to start for beginners.

Focus on Parable or Story Studies

Spend time looking at the meaning of one incident. Ask questions such as: "Who wrote this? To whom? When? Why? What type of literature is it? What is the whole passage about? What was originally intended for the first hearers? What does it say to us today?"

Roleplay Passages

Assign people to each character in a given story or incident. Let them act it out or read their own parts and discuss the feelings of each person. Encourage them to think about what others saw and heard or to share insights that might relate to the story. Most stories have many players, and each offers something significant.

Interpret Anew; Update the Language

Rewrite a parable for a modern setting. What would the parable of the Good Samaritan sound like if Jesus appeared at the typical high school and was trying to make a point to the average teenager?

Study by the Chapter or by the Book

Do a short-term study of one of the Gospels, one of Paul's letters, or a history book from the Old Testament. Ask similar questions to those listed under "Focus on Parable or Story Studies" (above).

Focus on Word Studies

Look at every instance of a word, such as the word *spirit*, examining the context, the nuance, and the root of each of the uses. This is interesting work for those interested in more in-depth Bible study.

Encourage Inductive Bible Studies

Use the following types of questions:

- Observation questions: requires facts in the response.
- Interpretation questions: requires analysis of the facts in a response.
- Application questions: requires displaying a personal grasp of the analysis in the response.

Discuss the Sunday Sermon

Don't overlook the Sunday sermon and its scriptural foundation as a Bible study class. This is not to criticize or to recast the sermon, but to seek deeper meaning and relevance for daily life.

These are just a few ways to look at the Bible. There are hundreds of activities and approaches to help bring this cornerstone of our faith to life. In taking the Bible seriously remember always to study it in context, asking not only what it says, but also what it means.

Being a people of the Bible means working hard to understand its central truths and learning to tell the story to others. Students of the Bible are called on to think, study, and reason. Our purpose is not to worship a book, something people call bibliolatry. We worship a living and dynamic God, and we learn of God though this book. Our faith rests squarely in Christ; being firmly rooted in that relationship allows us to deal honestly and deeply with the whole Bible. Bible study is not an end in itself. It is a means of our becoming what God would have us become.

Bible Study Tools

Bible Dictionary

A Bible dictionary is a reference book that alphabetically lists significant terms and names found in the Bible and gives a great deal of helpful information about people, places, and events. Some volumes include definitions and explanations of major theological concepts and doctrines, as well as articles on history, archaeology, and geography. Many have cross-references, maps, illustrations, and pronunciation guides.

Bible Commentary

A Bible commentary offers explanations and interpretations of the Bible, verse by verse, book by book. Most include a summary of each book, listing what scholars know about the history, authorship, date and background of the text. There also is usually some sort of everyday life application of the texts to help clarify the meanings and to give a jump-start on a devotion or chapel talk.

Concordance

A concordance is an alphabetical index of primary words found in the Bible. For example, if you were looking for the story of "that widow who did something with a coin," but didn't know where to begin, a concordance can help. You begin by thinking of the key words you can remember. In this instance it's the word *widow.* You can look up the word, and the concordance lists everywhere this word occurs in the Bible. The listings show the word in a sentence fragment, followed by the book, chapter, and verse, so you can quickly find the one you're looking for.

Concordances also help with word studies. If you were studying the word *prayer,* you could look it up in a concordance, and it would direct you to every instance it's used in the Bible.

For More Help

The Upper Room publishes a bi-monthly devotional magazine for youth titled *Devo'zine.* Each issue contains meditations, Scripture, prayers, articles, and reflection questions. Special savings are available for orders of ten or more copies. Their website is **www.upperroom.org/devozine**.

Starting With the Old Testament, by Stephen Travis. Published by Abingdon Press. Available through Cokesbury (800-672-1789).

Starting With the New Testament, by Stephen Travis. Published by Abingdon Press. Available through Cokesbury (800-672-1789).

Teaching the Bible to Adults and Youth, by Dick Murray and Lyle E. Schaller. Published by Abingdon Press. Available through Cokesbury (800-672-1789).

Introducing the Bible, by William Barclay. Published by Abingdon Press. Available through Cokesbury (800-672-1789).

Chapter

What Does a Youth Group Do?

What About Programs?

There is a good deal of talk today about the demise of program-oriented ministry. An alternative such as people-oriented planning or some type of more personal-sounding model is usually suggested. The issue here is an important one and needs to be clearly stated.

We all have, do, and will continue to do programs! Whatever name we give to our focus for gathering youth—people-oriented, worship-centered, discipleship-focused, need-based, ministry-motivated, or Christ-centered—the basic fact remains that most result in some form of program.

However, whenever planning is focused on filling a block of time with lots of activity for the sake of activity, giving little consideration to whom we're dealing with and what we're trying to accomplish, it becomes unlikely that spiritual growth will occur. This kind of fuzzy focus results in less-than-productive ministry programs. Conversely, when planning is done with prayerful consideration of the needs of youth from a Christian perspective, the program can become a ministry opportunity to help youth grow as disciples.

What Should Happen When Youth Meet?

Youth Leadership

A youth group should be a place where youth develop leadership skills. The emphasis is on helping youth learn and practice leadership skills, rather than on creating and implementing good programs. The process is more important than the product. One reason many youth drop out of youth ministry may be that they are not being challenged or trusted to be leaders.

Sanctuary

Youth ministry should provide a safe space for youth to talk to each other. Just as play is the "work" of children, talking is the work of youth. This should be a place where youth can wrestle with new and old values, roles, and beliefs. John Wesley spoke of holy conversation or Christian conferencing as a means of receiving God's grace.

Every youth gathering event would benefit from including structured and unstructured time. As explained above, time for talking is crucial. There should be enough unstructured time to allow youth to talk freely, yet enough structured time so that youth can focus their talk on a selected topic or experience. Well-prepared structured time helps youth sense that something important is happening.

When Do Groups Meet?

Effective UMY groups meet regularly, preferably weekly, for specific events chosen by the group members to suit their particular needs and schedules. Sunday evening is one typical time. However, other groups meet on weeknights or on Saturday afternoons. Don't be afraid to experiment with times. As ministries grow, there may be several different gatherings of youth for different reasons in any given week. Gatherings could include a Wednesday night Bible study, a Monday morning breakfast prayer group, a Sunday afternoon music/drama group, or a Tuesday after-school tutoring program. All should target different youth interested in different Christian themes with varying goals. Whatever the time, reason, or audience, choose to meet the interests of those interested, and you will accomplish what you have planned.

Age-Level Groupings

If possible, a congregation's ministry with youth should provide at least two age-level groups (traditionally junior high and senior high). Concerns, interest, and abilities vary greatly from the youngest seventh grader to the most mature twelfth grader. Attempting to combine a wide age range into one group usually will result in losing participants. Churches with large numbers of youth and a variety of programs may require three or more groups for effective ministry.

Junior high youth usually will be denied opportunities for leadership development if they are in the same group with senior high youth. By having their own group, junior highs will gain the confidence and skill to reach their potential as leaders. Your senior high ministries will benefit as junior highs, with exposure to leadership in their own setting, graduate into the senior high group.

Try to work toward at least two groups before it seems necessary, even if there are only two youth at each age level. Each ministry can then grow by fostering the specific interests and abilities of the younger and older youth. If you have small numbers of youth, consider joining forces with a neighboring church or with a cluster of churches in order to have two age groups. Effective ministries have existed with no more than six to twelve active participants split into separate learning times while still doing other activities together as one larger group.

Look to community school structures for guidance on how to group youth. Grade divisions in your schools suggest a logical way to organize youth ministries along age-level lines. For example, if you have a middle school that groups sixth and seventh graders together, that grouping might work well for your church.

What Should We Do?

Traditionally youth ministry was organized to address ministry through five areas. These categories could be woven into each gathering in small ways or, taken one by one, could become the focus of an entire gathering.

1. Fellowship—times to get to know, interact with, and care for one another.
2. Service—times to live our faith in the congregation and community.
3. Worship—times to praise God.
4. Study/Discussion—times to reflect together on the content and meaning of the gospel and other chosen topics.
5. Outreach—times to reach out to others in order to be a growing community of believers.

These areas are still helpful as building blocks for discipleship, giving youth a variety of opportunities to express their response to God's grace. Attention to these areas can yield a balanced and healthy overall ministry.

Common Components of Youth Meetings

Every congregation will have its own approach to its youth ministries. You will need to evaluate the strengths and gifts of your congregation, consider the needs of your youth, and craft a style all your own. This is the beauty of how God moves in our various communities and of what God leads us to be and do. The following are offered only as components of a suggested schedule. Putting them together in helpful and creative ways that fit your arena is still a task that needs to be addressed by all involved in the youth ministry of your church.

1. Gathering Time (about 10 minutes)

People tend to trickle into events, and youth are no different. This makes beginning a key activity on time difficult. As soon as you start something, invariably a few more kids show up. The new ones don't know what's going on, and if you try to stick them quickly into the activity, it can mean restarting or confusing what is already happening. Combat this by planning a brief gathering activity that allows people to drift in without complicating things for the ones who are already present.

Larger groups may offer several activity options, allowing youth to self-select according to their own comfort level.

2. Announcement/Business (5 to 10 minutes)

This is the time to promote upcoming events, report on past activity, clarify who will do what at the next event, and so forth. Keep this short, making sure it doesn't become your main purpose for gathering.

3. Main Program (up to 30 minutes)

When a program theme is selected, approach it in different ways using different methods. Don't make the mistake of trying to focus on several different ideas in the course of one program. Use recreation, discussions, Scripture, and so forth to highlight various aspects of one main theme.

4. Movement (15 to 20 minutes)

Movement means activity, games, and fun. Don't make the mistake of thinking movement only means playing a competitive game. Not all people have been blessed with graceful athletic control of their bodies, so consider how your selection will affect the participants. Perhaps providing concurrent alternatives can accommodate everyone's abilities.

5. Devotions/Worship (5 to 20 minutes)

The depth and length of this section is heavily dependent on the faith maturity of your teens. Realize that your audience may change from week to week as well. Some groups are singing groups, and they enjoy the celebration of music or liturgical movement and look forward to this part in their discipleship walk. Other groups simply roll their eyes and wonder how long this will last. Don't force it; work with it.

6. Meals (15 to 20 minutes)

Question: How long does it take an average teen to eat three slices of pizza and find the bottom of his or her glass? About as long as it took you to read that question! Feeding youth when they are in a group is an option that should be thought through. Questions to ask: "Is it necessary? When will the food be served? Who prepares, serves, cleans up?"

A Typical Sunday Evening Schedule

Movement/Community Building/Gathering—20 minutes.
Program—30 minutes.
Joys and Concerns Prayer Circle—5 to 10 minutes.
Closing Worship or Meditation—10 minutes.
Business—5 to 10 minutes.
UMY Benediction.

Or:

Snack Supper for All Youth—15 to 20 minutes.
Around-the-Tables Activity and Singing—10 to 15 minutes.
Program (separate for junior and senior high)—30 minutes.
Business—5 to 10 minutes.
Closing Song and/or Prayer.
UMY Benediction.

Or:

Middle High Youth Meet—30 minutes.
Meal With All Youth—15 minutes.
Brief Mixer With All Youth—30 minutes.
Senior High Youth Meet—5 to 10 minutes.

These three examples assume that you have at least an hour and a half for your UMY meeting. If you have less time, you will have to be more selective. Always allow adequate time for the main activity (generally called the program), which focuses on the purpose of the gathering. Make every effort to limit the business portion of the meeting to no more than five or ten minutes. Lengthy business sessions are not compatible with the purposes of United Methodist youth ministry.

Special Events

Occasionally a particular special event will dictate its own time frame, perhaps excluding all parts of the regular schedule other than the program itself. Such programs can provide variety and change, perhaps appealing to youth who may not have attended your group previously. These programs can be excellent opportunities for special invitations of outreach to new and inactive group members. The following are just suggestions:

- Going to the local television or radio station and meeting with the program director to discuss the standards that are considered when a change is made in the schedule.
- Attending a special worship in a different location, such as on top of a mountain, in a boat, in a funeral home chapel, or around a fire.
- Planning an outdoor "Crazy Olympics" complete with teams, streamers, funny events, gag prizes, and lots of laughs.
- Having a simulation activity that deals with values and decision-making processes, followed by a discussion on what the participants learned as they played.
- Serving takeout barbecue chicken dinner as a fundraising event.
- Painting furniture and repairing toys for a church's weekday preschool (if not your own, another church in the community).
- "Attacking" a selected area of your community with garbage bags to pick up litter.

Planning a Session

Whether you are planning a special program or a regular UMY meeting, the following questions are helpful.

- What is the program topic, and how will it be developed?
- How will we publicize and promote it?

- Who is responsible for each aspect of the program?
- Are the required resources on hand?
- Who will secure them?
- How much time will be needed for each part of the program?
- Has recreation been planned? Who is in charge?
- Is worship included? Who is in charge?
- What schedule (flexible, please) do we need to follow?
- What announcements need to be made?
- How will the session be guided?
- How will the leadership be shared?
- Are the facilities in order (room arrangement, heating/cooling requirements, supplies, and so forth)?
- Have all assignments been carried out?
- Are there any other details that need to be handled?
- How will we evaluate this program? How will we know if our goals were accomplished?

Combining Age Groups

For programs where all ages will be together:

- Gear the comprehension level more toward the junior high youth than the senior high youth. Some stretching is good for younger youth, but comprehension expectations should be realistic.
- Select program topics with broad appeal. For example, a program on colleges is not highly relevant to seventh and eighth graders.
- Adapt the total time spent on content sessions toward the junior high youth's capacity. Younger youth do not take so readily to hour-long discussions.
- Use a variety of methods.
- Keep content on the more concrete side; junior high youth usually do not handle abstract discussions as well as senior high youth.

For programs where part of the presentation is made to the group as a whole, with discussion taking place in two smaller groups divided along age-level lines:

- Focus the content presentation at a ninth grade level.
- Devise separate questions for the groups, making them appropriate for the different age levels.
- Have an adult advisor for each group.

Attitudes of Youth Leaders

Attitude is the paintbrush that colors absolutely everything with which it comes into contact. Look for the good, and you'll find it. Look for the bad, and you will see it every time. If it's all present around us anyway, and choice is our decision, why not look for, encourage, and nurture the good? Here are a few ideas.

- Expect all who attend to make a positive difference in your life.
- Listen to other people; make an effort to really hear what they are saying.
- Participate in the various activities with the group.
- Respect other people, including those who don't agree with some of your ideas.
- Desire to make your ministry all that it is capable of becoming.
- Assume program and activity responsibilities when asked, with a willingness to volunteer without being asked.
- Spread enthusiasm that is contagious.
- Express Christian caring through courteous and supportive behavior.
- Commit yourself to make youth ministry a high priority in your life, supporting it with your regular attendance, abilities, and prayers.
- Believe God invites us to seek love and justice for all people as a normal expression of our Christian faith.

Be sure not to bring:
- A tendency to form exclusive cliques within the group.
- Leftovers from arguments at or about school(s).
- Tendency to ridicule or put down others.
- Inattentiveness in the midst of programs, games, and projects.
- The temptation to exclude those whom you are not already friends with or those whom for some other reason you tend to ignore.

Building Community

Relationships are the primary energizing force in the lives of most adolescents. Relationships provide us with trusted friends with whom to discuss important questions such as, "Who am I?" and "Am I okay?" or "Do you like me?" Community building is a process of assisting youth in forging such relationships, not only with other youth and adults, but also with God. Community building may be the single most crucial task of youth ministry.

- Community requires an atmosphere of patience, persistence, and commitment. Community cannot be forced or socially engineered. It is developed through the sharing of ideas and insights and through personal revelation.
- Community is built through team activities such as decision-making, problem solving, strategizing, and consensus building.
- Community requires contribution. Each person must be willing to take an active role in the creation of something he or she values. Youth need to see that their gifts and talents contribute to a whole that is greater than any individual in the community of faith.
- Communication is an important factor in the formation of community. Talking and sharing ideas is a way we develop trust between ourselves and others. As trust deepens, levels of intensity and intimacy grow, and friendships are developed.
- In Christian community, youth find freedom and security. With freedom and security comes a willingness to reveal more of the self, knowing it will bring support and encouragement, not criticism or judgment. A sense of community, which celebrates both individuality and commonality, will compel youth to understand a Christ who encourages and embraces us with unconditional love and acceptance.

Guidelines for Building Community

Community Respects Individual Needs

Community building must respect individual needs. Just as we each have a preferred style of learning, we also have a preferred style of interacting with people. Working at community building is a group process. Some youth are more comfortable with groups and processes than others. Some people just need more time.

Effectiveness Is Affected by Size

Effectiveness in community building is related to size. It has been noted that the best unity happens in small groups. When small groups nurture community, their work influences what happens in larger groups.

Community Building Is Focused on Christ

Time must be spent understanding, modeling, and anticipating Christlike behaviors. Community is built on the principles of Christian faith—God's grace is available to all; God created and loves us all; God calls us to love and serve all.

Community Is Built Through a Variety of Experiences

Games, projects, discussion, worship, singing, preparing meals, and eating together are just a few experiences that can help build community.

Community Is as Unique as the Persons Who Form It

Arriving at the right plan for building community in your youth ministry will take time, effort, thought, and discussion. It will require prayer, meditation, Bible study, and thoughtful discernment. Done effectively, community building will have a profound spiritual impact on all your church's youth. Trust God for insight and wisdom. Trust yourselves to listen and to find ways to meet needs. God will bless your efforts and your results.

Recreation

Recreation is critical in your planning because it is the point of entry for many youth. When a newcomer attends, he or she will quickly learn about the faith of your group by the way group members engage in recreation.

Recreation literally means to recreate, revitalize, or make new. Recreation can revitalize your group's learning about God and Christian community. Because playing involves doing, it is a primary method for learning facts and attitudes. Observe how group members treat each other during recreation. It will communicate more about how they value others than will any program on this subject.

Avoid games that:

- Make one or more persons the brunt of a joke, even a good-natured, regularly attending youth who can "handle" it. These activities can threaten shy and self-conscious youth who are frightened they may be the next victim. Don't create teams by choosing sides, because someone always has to be chosen last.
- Focus on cutthroat competition.
- Involve needless destruction of property, even if it is material purchased for destruction. Think through the subtle message that is being taught and the values being communicated.
- Use food wastefully.
- Create a group of "rejected" persons on the sidelines.
- Pit boys against girls.
- Pit individuals against each other.

Use games that:
- Build trust among participants.
- Stress cooperation in order to accomplish a goal.
- Develop a sense of unity and Christian community.
- Are noncompetitive.
- Enable membership on the teams to change.
- Communicate that individuals are more important than the game.
- Allow everyone to play, including the person with a disability, the youngest person, and the oldest person present.

Music

Don't isolate music to a choir or to worship times; make it part of all that you do in your youth ministry. Incorporate music into opening and closing rituals. Create sacred space with it. Use music as a tool. Use it for fun. Use music after snacks and before announcements. Use it as a transition from one idea to another.

Setting aside a music time may mark it as different from the rest of the youth ministry setting and may allow youth who are uninterested in music to blow it off and to see music as unimportant.

Plan program time to discuss what role music plays in the lives of teens. Talk about lyrics; let youth share their thoughts and favorites; and explore different types of music to broaden horizons.

Bring in a musician who can offer insights and direction.

Please note that groups wanting to photocopy song sheets or songbooks that include copyrighted material must get written permission from the publishers for each song reproduced. This obligation applies to all copyrighted material, not just to music. Your church should provide responsible and ethical leadership in this matter. Negotiating such permission is not an option; it's an obligation with legal consequences.

Worship

Worship is the one experience that distinguishes youth ministry from other activities in the lives of youth. Youth can have experiences of study, fellowship, service, and even outreach in other school or community groups; yet only in youth ministry will they have the opportunity to worship. In spite of this uniqueness, worship often receives the least attention. Why? Perhaps we have assumed that worship is our pastor's responsibility or that attendance at the Sunday morning worship service is sufficient. Or perhaps we have limited youth worship to a special event around a campfire during a retreat.

Worship can be the primary means for your youth to realize the worth or importance of God in their lives. The lives of youth are filled with many distractions and activities, leaving little time for quiet reflection. Therefore, a prime role of worship in youth ministry is to help youth become focused and aware of God's presence and to connect to that presence.

Worship should undergird all we do. Every event can become an occasion for worship. Sacred space can be established by dimming the lights and sitting in a circle with a lighted candle and other symbols of our faith (as appropriate to the occasion) in the center. Reflection on the topic of study, recreational event, service project, or special occasion can then occur spontaneously or through prepared liturgies written by youth themselves. This vision of worship is different from pre-planned "sit down, it's time to be holy" devotions imposed on the youth by one or two leaders. The most powerful worship experiences will be ones that youth create and lead themselves, out of their own experiences.

The United Methodist Youth Benediction

The UMY Benediction has been a standard closing ritual for many UMY groups for many years. Group members stand in a circle, crossing their right arms over their left arms, and then joining hands. Speaking aloud, the youth repeat Numbers 6:24-26. After saying "Amen," group members raise up their arms, turn to their right, and face outward while continuing to hold hands.

In the closing circle, facing each other with arms crossed and hands held, the group is tightly knitted together, symbolizing the sense of closeness and the singleness of purpose and heart that binds them together in Christ. However, as disciples all are called to go into the world facing outward with arms open wide. So at the conclusion of the prayer, all turn to face the world. This new posture symbolizes going into the world as ambassadors of God's grace, justice, and truth, with heart, arms, and eyes open. Though the group is not as tight as it was moments before, all are still "in touch" with one another and with the faith that binds them until God brings them together again.

The LORD bless you and keep you;
the LORD make his face to shine upon you, and be gracious to you;
the LORD lift up his countenance upon you, and give you peace.
(Numbers 6:24-26)
Amen.

For More Help

CCLI (Christian Copyright Licensing, Inc.): 17201 Northeast Sacramento St., Portland, OR 97230; phone: 800-234-2446. This is a licensing company for over 2,500 music publishers. Securing a license from CCLI allows a church to copy items for congregational use, including printing in orders of service and on overhead transparencies.

Connecting to God: Nurturing Spirituality Through Small Groups, by Corrine Ware. Published by Alban Institute.

Chapter

8

What About Service?

Service Is Foundational

For a group of youth and adults becoming disciples, service is foundational. Through youth ministry we do the work of Christ. We are called to be in ministry, "to put feet to our faith."

With God's grace, we dare to respond to the challenge of Matthew 25:40—"Truly I tell you, just as you did it to one of the least of these who are members of my family, you did it to me."

Service is a natural, necessary expression of faith in Christ, of becoming a disciple. Being in service to others does not make us special or deserving of favors. This avenue of ministry is simply what we are called to do—from love, in love—as the people of God.

How do we integrate reflection and learning with service? Service learning can take many forms. Keep these points in mind as you choose and carry out your ministry of service.

1. When selecting a service project, don't make assumptions about who needs help and what type of help is needed. This can be insulting, even when intentions are well-meaning. Being asked to help is more important and should be the only entrance into doing mission work.

2. All those interested in a service opportunity should share in the work of developing the service activity, planning the details, and reflecting on that work.

3. Inventory the skill level of those youth who are interested. Those interested need to be truly able to do the work required. Can this be an opportunity to involve adults with special skills in your congregation or community?

4. Genuine commitment to the task is critical. To carry the project through to completion, conscientious work and faithful attendance at work sessions will be required. People will be counting on you to finish what you begin.

5. Nurture caring, not condescending, attitudes toward those served. Christian service springs from Christian love that is not patronizing. It does not congratulate itself, nor does it parade around saying, "Oh, you poor people, look what we nice youth are doing for you." We may not always be greeted with reciprocal openness and respect, but that is not the issue. Negative responses should never deter us from Christian caring.

6. The project should be within your budget ability. Be sure you can meet the project's monetary requirements.

7. Consider time required versus time youth can realistically give.

8. Responsible reflection occurs before, during, and after the project. Some reflection questions include:
   • Is this particular project a genuine need we are invited to meet?
   • What are some of the facts related to this need?
   • What biblical insights prepared us to go in the spirit of Christ?
   • Did we need specialized help from others?
   • What happened to us in the midst of the project?
   • How would we describe our own working relationships?
   • Did any of our feelings change as we worked?
   • How would we evaluate the activity?
   • What Biblical images or stories does the work remind us of?
   • What were the strengths of what we did?
   • What were some weaknesses in what we did?
   • If we had it to do over again, what project elements would we keep? Which ones would we change?

Finally, remember to consider and to discuss the real reasons why you want to serve others. Serving is a way of understanding Christ and Christ's mission on earth. Serving is a way of connecting faith with life. Serving is a lifestyle choice, not a one-time enterprise. Don't serve to alleviate guilt or to feel better about yourself. Don't serve to be appreciated or applauded. Serve because Christ served others. Serve because it is the right thing to do. Serve because you want to live your faith and not just talk about it.

Service Ministry in the Congregation

Here are a few examples of how youth can minister through service to their own church. In choosing activities, base the service on genuine needs. Never twist service into busy work, or see it as an end in itself (done just so you can say you did something).

In the church program and around the building:
- Cleanup.
- Yard work.
- Fix-up and repair.
- Ushering.
- Regular maintenance.
- Office work.
- Running errands.
- Painting.
- Food preparation.
- Developing and maintaining a church website.

Service ministry to congregation members:
- Emergency housekeeping.
- Yard work.
- Transportation.
- Friendship calls.
- Visiting the sick and people who have limited ability to leave home.
- Running errands.

Service Ministry to the Local Community

Begin by partnering with existing organizations. More care needs to be exercised as youth go forth into an arena less acquainted with the church and Jesus Christ. Possibilities include:
- Programs at healthcare facilities.
- Programs for older adults, including those at retirement homes.
- Programs for children.
- Meals on Wheels program.
- Red Cross activities.
- Gleaning.
- Soup kitchens.

- Shelters for homeless or battered persons.
- Home repair work camps.
- Habitat for Humanity.
- Teaching literacy.
- Tutoring.
- Other needs in your community can be found by calling your local United Way or by looking under "social services" in your telephone book.

Service Ministry Beyond the Local Community

This level involves the highest level of advanced planning. This requires more skill and a much longer lead time to get the details worked out and lined up. A few possibilities include:

- Regional and national work camps.
- Relief and disaster assistance.
- Rebuilding after disaster.
- Hunger programs.

Long-distance service opportunities exist in abundance. Many organizations have been in the business of serving others for years. Some of the better publicized agencies rely on the word of mouth of those who have served with them. Check with other youth ministers in your area who have worked with these agencies. Ask for:

- A critique of the organizations with which they have worked.
- Candid reflections about positives and negatives.
- Costs involved with these projects: registration fees, room and board fees, donations of dollars and supplies, and transportation costs.
- The values and goals of individual organizations. Be aware that a portion of registration fees may be "for profit" and may be used to further causes unrelated to missions.

Service Ministry Through and With Others

Many people are already working with youth in your community: senior and junior high school principals, teachers, and guidance counselors; law enforcement officials; social workers; leaders in civic youth-serving organizations; parents and adults working with youth in other churches; and so forth. Join together with these to identify and to minister to the needs of youth in your community.

There are many ways to design service opportunities, both one-day projects and weeklong or longer events. Locally, you can volunteer as part of an organization's existing system. You can cooperate with other church youth groups or agencies to develop a joint effort. You can model your work after something that has already been proven effective. You can even create your own vision of service and put it into action.

There are several issues to consider when cooperating with existing organizations:

- Study the agency and know its values and goals. Make sure its values and goals match those of your denomination and your congregation.
- If either party is uncomfortable with the other, a relationship should not be formed.
- Assure the agency that any unusual expense incurred because of your involvement will be covered by your ministry.
- Insist that the work you are asked to do is not just "busy work." Expect that the work will be challenging and educational, and make sure the agency understands why.

Youth Service Fund

The Youth Service Fund (YSF) is money that is given by youth, administered by youth, and used to serve youth. However, YSF is more than simply raising money. YSF is a commitment made by United Methodist youth to those in need—in their own communities, across the United States, and around the world. Youth Service Fund is an opportunity to witness to the transforming love of Jesus Christ.

YSF is the only authorized United Methodist fund directly related to youth. It is the only fund over which youth have primary administrative control. It can truly be considered "second mile" giving, because it does not replace a young person's responsibility for giving to his or her local church program.

YSF benefits people in need. The money raised for YSF supports projects at the annual conference and national levels of The United Methodist Church. On both levels, YSF projects are carefully selected by a committee of youth and adult workers with youth. Each project must address the needs of youth in a concrete and effective manner. For example, YSF money has provided assistance for youth with disabilities, resources for counseling, support for youth centers, ministries to low-income neighborhoods, and training for career development.

Youth participating in YSF benefit from putting their faith into action as disciples and as stewards. Stewardship is an act of faithful, responsible use of all our resources—skills, time, energies, and money. The vows of church membership commit us to support The United Methodist Church with our prayers, our presence, our gifts, and our service. YSF provides one excellent way of making good that commitment.

How does the Youth Service Fund work? Money is raised by youth in a church and is sent to the treasurer of the annual conference. (Your pastor can give you the name and address.) Seventy percent of the money is retained in the annual conference. Of that money at least one third goes to projects within the conference, at least one third goes to projects outside the conference, and one third may be used for YSF education and administration.

Thirty percent of the money raised is sent to the National Youth Ministry Organization of The United Methodist Church to support projects across the United States and in foreign countries. Eighty percent of this amount goes to projects selected by the projects review committee of the steering committee. Twenty percent goes to education and administration.

Find out about the particular projects being sponsored by YSF in your conference and on the national level. Your group members will be more excited about raising and giving money when they know exactly where it is going. Is there a project ministering to the needs of youth in your community that needs funds? Has your UMYF wanted to start a community youth center, yet you don't have enough money? Apply to receive YSF funds from your annual conference, another annual conference, or NYMO.

How Can We Raise Money for YSF?

Individual Gifts

Learning to make an individual financial commitment to the church and its ministries is part of Christian stewardship of money. If every one of the approximately 600,000 United Methodist youth gave one penny a day, there would be $2,190,000 a year for YSF projects, education, and administration.

Pledges
- Set a definite goal for the amount your group wants to raise.
- Allow youth to decide for themselves how much they will give on a weekly basis. The cost of a candy bar or canned soft drink each day can add up to a large pledge.
- Establish a definite timeline for when the pledge period begins and when you will collect the money. You also may choose to design a worship service to dedicate the money received.

Fundraising Activities

If you choose to organize a fundraiser, plan one that is fun, safe, and provides a real service. Here are some examples:
- Work day: Rake leaves, clean garages, wash windows, paint fences, repair porches, caulk windows, mow yards—all for a fee that goes to YSF. Or advertise that your UMY members are available for a half or full day of free labor, with the persons who take the free labor making a donation to YSF for what the job was worth to them.
- Recycling center: Part of a Christian's response as a good steward has to do with saving and reusing resources. If you have a local outlet that buys used glass, aluminum, or paper, consider setting up a center where people can deposit these items. Whatever you are paid by the buyer(s) of the materials goes to YSF.
- Old favorites: These are the "tried and true" ways of raising money: car wash, rummage sale, spaghetti supper, pancake breakfast, bake sale, and so forth.

For More Help

A wide variety of mission opportunities are listed on the youth ministry pages of The General Board of Discipleship website: **www.gbod.org/youth.**

For more information about Youth Service Fund projects and promotional materials, write to your annual conference Council on Ministry or The National Youth Ministry Organization, P.O. Box 840, Nashville, TN 37202. (E-mail: NYMO@aol.com)

Chapter

Youth Ministry Is Congregational Ministry

Support of the Total Congregation

Youth ministry is not a substitute for church or a branch office of the main church. It is an integral part of the congregation, with its young members participating in the total life of the church, as well as participating in youth ministry. Likewise, a congregation should not view its youth ministry as something extra, or as a program off in the basement.

However, it's not unusual to see youth programs willingly marginalized within a congregation. The congregation is content with the youth being cared for, and the youth leadership is happy to have some breathing room. While this looks on the surface to be a win-win situation, the truth is, everyone loses.

Youth ministries that isolate themselves from the congregation result in unbalanced ministries. For many reasons, the connection between youth and the rest of the congregation should be solid and anchored at many different points.

Continuity

When we sequester our youth ministries away from normal congregational life, graduating youth never have a place to "come home to." They neither understand the local church nor know how to work within its culture. When or if, as young adults, they seek to reconnect with a congregation, they seek the only thing they know, the same kind of warm, fun, intimate worship experience they remember having in youth ministry. They enter a typical Sunday morning congregational worship and are quickly dismayed. Because they are unequipped to know how to integrate, work to change, or assess what they should do, they often quietly drop away. This should be a great concern to congregations.

Community

Youth ministry is best nurtured in the context of a community of faith that includes children, youth, and adults. When youth ministry functions outside the rhythm of church life, a critical connection to the community is lost.

Relationships

Adults have the responsibility to pass the faith to the next generation. Within the local family of faith are abundant opportunities for ministry, support, interaction with other generations, and other ways to develop long-term relationships benefiting youth and adults. Listening to and interacting with our elders, intentionally spending time with people who faced the challenges of adolescence, can be helpful for young people. The adults have chances to impart wisdom, nurture, and grace to searching youth.

Accountability

Everyone needs to have some level of accountability for his or her spiritual and discipleship practices, especially those in leadership positions. Busy leaders are tempted to neglect their spiritual mentors, to delay time-consuming study, and to omit third-party review of their thinking, actions, and intent. Where should you go for these things? The obvious and practical answer is the church to which the youth ministry belongs. Sunday school teachers, church staff, adult and youth accountability groups, parents, formal evaluations, task committees, lay leaders, and pastors are built-in guidance systems providing needed counsel in Christian discipleship.

Gaining Congregational Support

High visibility of youth in the congregation is one key to gaining the congregation's support for your youth ministry. Adults must see and hear youth so they can appreciate youth as people with valued ideas and gifts. Interaction between youth and the administrative council, the council on ministries, and various committees will encourage shared ministry. Such experiences of joint ownership in ministry can result in advocacy in the future. Through activities such as the examples that follow, you can enhance visibility and congregational/youth partnership:

- Sit together in the front pews during congregational worship.
- Take pictures during youth events and display them in prominent places in your church building.
- Volunteer to provide flowers for the altar once a quarter.
- Volunteer to help with secretarial duties in the church office.
- Write a column for your congregation's newsletter.
- Volunteer to give the children's sermon and to help with child-care as needed.
- Serve complimentary juice and muffins between Sunday school and worship.
- Serve on administrative groups in the congregation.
- Include youth in worship leadership (ushering, reading Scripture, greeting, leading prayers and creeds, and so forth).
- Make posterboard-sized get-well cards for church members in the hospital. Have the youth sign and, if possible, deliver the cards.
- Sponsor events that require entire church involvement, such as a church cleanup day or food drives for a local food bank.

Youth Serving on Committees and Boards

Youth can and should be encouraged to participate on committees and boards in the local church. While many churches faithfully name youth to these groups, that doesn't guarantee quality involvement. To make sure youth serve to their potential, review the following:

Plan Meetings When Youth Can Attend

Most meetings happen at times that are convenient for adults, not necessarily for youth. The net result is that youth just can't get there to participate. If regular meetings can't be adjusted to suit everyone's needs, perhaps an annual or quarterly meeting designed to get input from the youth could be arranged.

Select Youth Comfortably Capable of Interacting With Adults

Deciding which youth are nominated and placed on boards and committees is worthy of careful and prayerful thought.

Meet With Youth Members Immediately Before a Meeting

Take time to help youth understand the agenda and where any hot spots may be. Equip them for participation and reinforce their role and reason for being there.

Have Youth Report Back to Youth

Encourage youth members of committees and boards to report in youth gatherings on what happened and what they learned. Coach them through the reporting experience as well.

Improving Awareness of Youth Ministry

At times youth ministry is unintentionally overlooked by local church decision-makers. Why this happens isn't as important as what can be done to minimize it in the future. Examine the places in your local church where decisions are made: money matters in the finance committee, personnel matters in the pastor-parish committee, worship matters in the worship committee, and so forth.

Who among the adult committee members knows intimately what is going on week to week with the church's youth ministry? Is someone on the committee keeping the needs of youth, their concerns and their issues, before the group? Youth deserve representation at every level of the congregation. The two approaches listed below are most helpful when they are combined.

Outside In

Begin with the nominations committee. Select a person who is willing to serve on this committee and who knows the church members well enough to nominate people (youth and adults) for vacancies. Check with your pastor to discover if vacancies exist and what procedures are followed for filling them. Once a "youth-friendly" person is elected, he or she can prayerfully nominate those who, in addition to being faithful and skilled, also have the added dimension of being well-versed in the youth ministry of the church. This is slow, long-range planning, but it pays wonderful dividends later.

Inside Out

Review the names of adults on the boards and committees and begin actively involving and exposing them to the youth ministry. Invite them to attend programs, retreats, work projects, and so forth. Help them learn what is going on: the kids, their needs, and their issues. In this way, over time, you should be able to embrace the hearts and heads of decision-makers throughout the church system.

This isn't license to place adults in decision-making positions so they can agitate for youth ministry. That type of stance creates a backlash effect that does more harm than good. Rather, this is to assure that when youth issues come up in those meetings, someone is present to represent the youth ministry from a position of strength and firsthand knowledge.

For More Help

It Takes a Congregation: How to Gain Support for Youth (SkillAbilities for Youth Ministry). Published by Abingdon Press. Available through Cokesbury (800-672-1789).

Chapter

Encouraging Participation

Getting Youth Involved

"Now there are varieties of gifts, but the same Spirit; and there are varieties of services, but the same Lord; and there are varieties of activities, but it is the same God who activates all of them in everyone. To each is given the manifestation of the Spirit for the common good. To one is given through the Spirit the utterance of wisdom, and to another the utterance of knowledge according to the same Spirit, to another faith by the same Spirit, to another gifts of healing by the one Spirit, to another the working of miracles, to another prophecy, to another the discernment of spirits, to another various kinds of tongues, to another the interpretation of tongues. All these are activated by one and the same Spirit, who allots to each one individually just as the Spirit chooses." (1 Corinthians 12:4-11)

Youth aren't a great deal different than anyone else when it comes to being motivated. They are subconsciously asking four questions:

Am I Needed?

I know many youth leaders who want more youth to get involved. Being wanted is nice, but it's not enough. Youth, like anyone else, gravitate to where they are needed, where a significant role is waiting for them.

Am I Expected?

Youth are looking for tangible signs that they're in the right place. Did you remember their names? Can you recall what significant concerns you last talked about? Can you stop what you're doing to go and greet them?

Am I Able to Help Lead?

Have there been adequate times for youth input in the youth ministry planning? Are the youth doing as much of the leadership work as possible?

Do They Like Me?

If teens feel that they are liked, by other youth and adults, they'll be back time after time. If they are uncertain whether or not they are liked, their commitment begins to equivocate. If they are aware that they are not liked or accepted, they will do one of two things: leave and not come back, or come back often and make as much trouble as they can manage.

Incorporating New Youth

Make your group the kind of place where people feel welcome and want to be. Consider the following questions:

- Is the spirit of Christ reflected in the attitudes and behaviors of everyone present?
- Are youth in visible positions of leadership?
- Are youth encouraged and supported in their ideas and comments?
- Is there time for the youth to talk freely without too much direction?
- Is there time for the youth to talk about specific topics in a safe, nonjudgmental arena?
- Do you take care to mix different youth up in small discussion/activity groups to enhance their ability to get acquainted with others?
- Do the youth who attend regularly know how to welcome newcomers?
- Are the skills and abilities everyone brings to the setting being used?
- Are new people invited to subsequent activities?
- Is your meeting place as attractive and as inviting as possible?

Planning For Maximum Involvement

Through planning, youth can feel ownership of what is going on. With ownership comes a sense of responsibility to make sure the plans are implemented. The number-one way to enable youth to stay motivated and to follow through on responsibilities is to let them help plan and choose activities for which they will be responsible.

Planning means:
- Seeing where you are.
- Deciding where God wants you to go.
- Moving a step at a time to reach your destination.

Inviting Youth

Invitations are important. As you invite youth to participate, keep these points in mind:

- Be specific: Make the invitation specific to the individual and a particular date or event. Don't simply tell each youth when to come or where to go; ask each one when he or she wants to be picked up, and plan to stay with him or her throughout the time.
- Be persistent: You will probably need to invite friends more than once.
- Be realistic: Your group members may receive a number of rejections before someone accepts the invitation. Don't take rejections personally and don't give up!
- Make invitations authentic and compelling. As you extend your invitations, you will be sharing good news, doing evangelism in a natural and effective way.
- Be clear about values and goals: Some youth will be more interested in what your ministry is trying to accomplish than in your recreational activities.

Inviting Unknown Youth

This invitation can be more difficult. Identify someone who has had some background experience with the person to be invited, such as a class at school or the same sports team. Pay special attention to youth who have just moved to your community. They probably will be experiencing some loneliness and would appreciate your invitation and offer of friendship.

Remember that in youth ministry we are called to be faithful, not successful. We must give our best and trust God for the outcome: The one who plants and the one who waters really do not matter. It is God who matters because God makes the plant grow: "So neither the one who plants nor the one who waters is anything, but only God who gives the growth . . . For we are God's servants, working together; you are God's field, God's building" (1 Corinthians 3:7, 9).

Working With Busy Youth

How do we address personal busyness, schedules of volunteers and participants, conflicting activities, academic schedules, rehearsals, practices, sports, clubs, and an attitude that we should try to do it all?

One obvious answer is to offer youth the one thing that no one else can: peace, stillness, and quiet. Youth ministries can offer opportunities for stillness without having to think through, explain, or account for their thoughts. Youth ministries can offer space, place, relationships, and acceptance. Youth ministry can be driven by a vision of Christ, who is more than willing to take our yoke of busyness and give us a lasting peace. What are some practical ways this can be done?

Accept Limitations

There are limitations and realities in our present day and age. We cannot fight true busyness. Instead, we must learn to work with it. No matter what event or activity we might have, what meeting we intend to hold, someone is going to have a conflict. What do we do? Cancel? No. If only two show—don't cancel. Take the two and have the best time possible, "... For where two or three are gathered in my name, I am there among them" (Matthew 18:20).

Know the Calendars

While it is impossible to anticipate every conflict, you can often avoid major ones by looking at school, family, and church calendars far in advance. Consider changing the camping trip that conflicts with a Scholastic Aptitude Test weekend and go for an "After SAT" party instead. This gives youth an excellent way to talk about taking the test, which is what's on their mind anyway.

Create Alternatives

In obvious situations, think about alternatives. Have the concert on a Saturday night or a Sunday afternoon. What you need to avoid is competing head to head with regular activities that involve the majority of youth you are attempting to serve. Forcing kids to make unnecessary and difficult choices isn't fair or helpful. Everyone loses—you, the kids, and other volunteers. This becomes especially difficult for parents who feel that poor planning is happening.

Know Your Audience

Relationships with youth and volunteers are the most important considerations in dealing with busyness. There is no substitute for knowing what they struggle with and then supporting them through it. Work with them in this godly process; support them faithfully, and expect good things to grow as a result. Face struggles fairly and courageously, and trust that all things will work for the good and the glory of God.

For More Help

Open Doors, Open Arms: How to Reach New Youth (SkillAbilities for Youth Ministry). Published by Abingdon Press. Available through Cokesbury (800-672-1789).

Chapter

What About Money?

Handling Money for Youth Ministry

For many, dealing with money and budgets is one of the most frustrating aspects of youth ministry. Here are a few recommendations for dealing with money matters.

Establish Procedures for Handling Money

All cash and checks for any event or activity should be deposited into the main church treasury account. This assures that all funds, receipts, and expenditures are in order. There are other kinds of accounting procedures. Some use separate checkbooks, or youth workers handle their budgets with special credit cards. The best checks and balances system, however, is to work with the church's treasury. In this way, most questions that might arise are well on their way to being answered before they're even asked.

Don't Make Budget the Barometer of Your Youth Ministry

Amazing ministry is accomplished with little or no cash. Don't let a lack of budget be a distraction from doing what you feel God is calling you to do. Focus on solutions to problems and needs, instead of how much money you do or don't have. Identify ideas that serve your target audience. Next, ask around to find if anyone else is already performing or offering the opportunities you're considering. If they are being offered, don't reinvent the wheel; pitch in instead!

Be Proactive at Budget Planning Time

Some suggest that a budget based on $100 per participating youth is a good budget request. In most United Methodist churches budgets are submitted in late summer or early fall. This is when finance campaigns and committees begin to work on a budget for the next calendar year. Never assume that church members know what kinds of things are going on in the youth program, and never assume that they will want to increase church support through budget increases. Be proactive! Demonstrate that the money is well-administered and well-accounted for, and thus maximize the chance of further support.

Explore a Variety of Ways to Pay for Ministry

Mobilizing all kinds of resources—monetary and material, as well as human—is essential to good problem solving. However, since this section of the handbook is about money, we'll focus on the dollars and cents. Once the annual budget is established and dollar amounts are certain, how else are resources generated to support trips, retreats, missions, scholarships, and special activities at the church?

- Self-supporting: Self-supporting means that those who are involved pay their own way. The total cost of an event is divided up among the paying participants.
- Fundraisers: Traditionally many churches have depended upon fundraisers to fund their youth ministries. Before you plan a fundraiser, check with your administrative council to see if the church has any policies regarding fundraisers.

Suggestions for Fundraisers

- Trade goods or services for cash. Offering to wash windows or cars, prepare food, or deliver greeting cards all have a common denominator in that there is a fair product in exchange for money earned.
- Hold a consignment sale. Don't get involved with a company that requires the youth group to purchase the goods first and then sell them. Look for agencies that allow you to sell their goods, such as pumpkins or Christmas trees, and then ship back what wasn't sold.
- Sell delivery services: hand deliver Christmas cards, valentine cards, or small trinkets. It's the personal approach that sells.
- Take donations for parent's night out, lawn work, window washing, spring or fall cleaning, pool cleaning, and pet sitting or walking.
- Hold "_____-a-thons" where pledges are committed for each segment completed, such as walking, baseball innings, rocking chair hours, bike miles, talking, cleaning, and raking.

- Plan a sale: bake, rummage, crafts, cookbooks, refreshments, birthday calendars, flowers, plants, eggs, stationery, pecans, T-shirts, or Sunday coffee, juice and muffins.
- Have a car wash. Sell tickets in advance, or take the car wash door to door.
- Have a free car wash. Secure pledges in advance for each car washed.
- Think food. Plan dinners such as spaghetti, pancake, or chicken; serve meals for ongoing groups in church such as United Methodist Women, senior citizens, and the children's choir; host a banquet or fish fry; or bring in barbecued chicken takeout. Don't forget special events such as Mother's Day and Father's Day.
- Plan an ice cream social.
- Hold a drive: paper, aluminum cans, bottles, and so forth.
- Conduct carnivals or fairs.
- Have a booth at local festivals.
- Set up refreshment stands at football games, Little League games, and so forth.
- Pre-sell pizzas or sub sandwiches, then make and deliver them ready to be frozen for use anytime.
- Plan dinner theater, concerts, or talent shows.
- Have yard sales or flea markets.
- Organize a Christmas gift-wrapping service.

Scholarships

Some parents or guardians don't have resources that allow their youth to participate even in basic activities. Be aware of such situations and be prepared to help. One primary way of assuring that everyone who wants to participate can do so is by providing scholarships. Administering scholarships can be tricky on a number of accounts.

Youth Who Need Help Will Not Ask for It

Youth will not ask for assistance because they've been taught that they don't need to take charity. Begin by taking the word *scholarship* out of the realm of charity and attach to it the word *work*. Call it a work grant. Set things up so money can be earned. Don't go overboard, though. Possibilities include:

- Helping with loading and unloading luggage for a retreat.
- Helping repack the food for an event.
- Helping with cleanup on the day after a big event.

Parents May Be Hesitant to Request

Conscientious people are sometimes reluctant to accept a free scholarship, as it might appear they're taking advantage of the situation. Everyone, regardless of his or her level of income, has a bad month from time to time. So present scholarships or work grants by suggesting that if this is a bad month, use a scholarship. Tell parents or guardians that if they can pay it back by the end of the year, the money will be gladly received; if not, that's fine.

How Much Do You Budget to Assist Unknown Numbers of Scholarships?

Start small and grow steadily. Establish a scholarship fund for the best and most important trip in a year. For example, set up two or three scholarships for an annual mission trip or the big spiritual life retreat. This is a beginning. If five people come forward to ask for assistance, sort it out. Maybe split the money evenly or find additional cash through a generous member of the congregation. The next budget year, you will have some experience on which to base your estimates.

Setting Up a Budget

A budget form should have enough information to sufficiently inform a reader of how much is being requested and for what general reasons. A budget will necessarily reflect each group's specific needs and programs, but there are general areas that shape what a typical budget looks like.

Materials Expenses

Estimate costs of providing all materials in a given year: curriculum, games, supplies, food and beverage, field trips, and so forth. Try establishing a general dollar amount for each week of ministry, such as ten dollars per week. Multiply this times the number of gatherings to get the total line item.

Events/Retreats and Trips

List each event or trip separately. Give the name or location of the event or trip and a cost estimate. List big-ticket items such as outside speakers, bands, transportation, lodging, food, materials, and equipment rental.

Depending upon the ministry you have planned, other budget categories might include:

- Recreation equipment.
- Entrance fees.
- Outreach.
- Insurance.
- Special one-time costs.
- Continuing education.
- Counselor training.

Regardless of the components or categories in a budget, be careful what information is included. Be clear about each item and how you present the plans and make the requests for funding. When a properly developed budget is presented, the recipients will see shared goals and visions represented. They will see items and costs blended with the visions of the whole community of faith. In a proper and carefully developed budget, the congregation will want to support the plan and the ministry opportunity it represents.

Retreats and Other Trips

What Makes Retreats Work?

What goes through people's minds when they hear the word *retreat*? Some think of cities, working in soup kitchens amid skyscrapers, parks, and museums. Others think of being miles from human development, with open skies, forests, campfires, and no television or telephones. Many imagine something in between those two extremes. Retreats continue to be one of the best ways to build Christian community. Regardless of the focus or theme, one of the wonderful, serendipitous benefits is how well trust and closeness develop individually, with others, and with God.

Consider the following reasons why retreats remain one of the most popular options with youth for developing and deepening discipleship.

New Surroundings

Getting away from the familiar and going to the unfamiliar has the effect of releasing teens from the normal roles they live in, day in and day out. In a new setting they have an option to relax, be themselves, and open up to the leading of the Holy Spirit.

A Captive Audience

Depending on the setting and intent of the retreat, there is an opportunity to have the undivided attention of a group for an extended period of time. This allows time not only for the introduction of a theme or idea, but also for many opportunities to reinforce learning in a short span of time.

Shared Community and Experiences

Youth are thrust into a setting with friends, people whom they know or at least share similar concerns and issues. This common bond heightens their willingness to be open to each other, deepening friendships, making new ones, and supporting one another in shared experiences. A shared history allows a group to develop. Retreats become stepping stones in the faith journey.

A Dozen Ingredients for a Successful Retreat

1. Identify a steering team of youth and adults to plan and to implement the event. Ideally, a few youth and an adult would be assigned to most of the categories listed below. If that is out of range for your size group, combine tasks to suit the number of available persons.

2. Decide on the purpose and goals of the outing. Ask, "Why have this retreat? Will it help us reach our target and move toward our vision? Will it move our youth in the direction we need to go?" Don't assume everyone has the same mental image of the purpose. Agreeing on an answer to these questions gets everyone on the same page: "We're going to retreat for the expressed purpose of . . ."

3. Promote the retreat. The rule of thumb is one month of promotion for each day of an event. Note that the "one month for each day of an event" rule only applies to promotion. Planning the dates, securing the location, signing up speakers and music, and so forth should be done months in advance. Produce publicity flyers, posters, bulletins, newsletter articles, and announcements. Parents or guardians should be specifically informed about what is required in the way of dates, times, financial support, encouragement, and applicable disciplinary measures. This task also includes developing a plan of registration. Decide when registration will open and close; what maximum and minimum number of persons can be accommodated; and where, when, and how the money is to be paid. Will payment be made by installments? Will it be made all at once? Make payment as convenient as possible for the participants.

4. Investigate sites and locations for the retreat. Opportunities run the gamut from the crowded beach blasts that cater to thousands to isolated mountain lodges. Wonderful things can happen in either setting. Which place depends on the ministry goals, the overall vision, and for whom and why the event is happening. One thing is clear: Don't get crossed up by mixing the right agenda

with the wrong location, or vice versa. Make sure the site and the goals work together. Follow up on issues such as:

- Sleeping arrangements.
- Meeting rooms.
- Recreation facilities.
- Meals (who fixes them and when and where will meals be eaten).
- Fees and hidden costs, such as phone call charges, towel fees, and firewood.
- Rules and expectations of the site management.

5. Develop a group behavior covenant. Before the trip is taken, have the youth write a covenant setting the standards for acceptable behavior and the consequences of breaking the covenant. The word *covenant* means "agreement" or "testament." In many Biblical passages a covenant is made that declares promises between God and the people—and the consequences if the promises are broken.

6. Inform the church and the parents. Make certain that your church officials understand the nature of the trip and give it their approval. Keep the church apprised of the group's whereabouts. A telephone call once the group has reached its destination is thoughtful. Publish the schedule of your trip or retreat in the church bulletin, newsletter, or as a bulletin insert. Ask members of your congregation to post the schedule on their refrigerators and to pray daily for your event. Parents need to be informed about the trip from registration until the travelers return home. They need to know the proposed itinerary, destination, and general activities; the address and telephone contact arrangements at the destination site and at en route lodgings; financial obligations; health and emergency release forms; which adults will accompany the youth; and the content of the group's covenant for conduct.

7. Determine the schedule. Tackle the schedule as soon as the theme is set. In what exact order will the retreat unfold and in what time frames?

8. Identify leadership. Identify those who will assume responsibility for the tasks listed on the schedule. Will you use a guest speaker? Who is responsible for worship? Do you need a music leader? Who will lead recreation? Who is responsible for planning and preparing food?

9. Identify and gather needed equipment. A master list of equipment is important. This list should include everything needed for recreation, program, worship, food, music, first aid, emergency lighting, and so forth. Keep space limitations of your vehicle(s) in mind.

10. Plan for emergencies. Secure an adequate first-aid kit and know how to use it; devise a health and liability form and make sure that the necessary forms for each participant are available at all times; make sure the group has adequate insurance coverage; locate the nearest hospital and medical help for major stopping points along the way; check for health hazards; establish fire exits; and set up a meeting spot for the group in case of disaster. Be aware of special health needs of participants (for example, juvenile diabetes or epilepsy), and obtain the services of a nurse for an extended outing. Follow your church's established policies for safety.

11. Make travel plans. This includes securing transportation; providing competent driver(s); giving travel directions; planning for side trips, if any; and planning for all stops. Break long rides with relaxation and recreation for both riders and drivers. The travel schedule should:
    • Reflect selected priorities.
    • Be realistic; don't try to cram too much in too little time—fatigue can be devastating to group dynamics.
    • Allow for changes when necessary and helpful.
    • Allow enough sleep time; resting in a moving vehicle is not the same as sound sleep between rides.
    • Be posted and given to participants in advance.

12. Evaluate and report the experience. Evaluation promotes celebration and leads to improvement. You can help the next group charged with planning a similar event by writing out in detail:
    • What went right and why.
    • What went wrong and why.
    • What you would recommend for similar events in the future.
    Multiply the value of the event by telling others what you learned and experienced during the event. This sharing also can encourage other groups to try similar activities. Sharing can be done with video presentations, posters displaying photographs, newsletter and newspaper articles, and so forth.

Many groups have a congregational dinner after their travel event to share words and pictures and what the event meant to them. The benefits of this kind of sharing are many: The congregation is informed about the "good news" of what is happening in the youth ministry; the youth gain support for their next endeavor; a powerful example is given to the children of the church about what youth ministry can be and what they have to look forward to; and youth have the opportunity to share their faith in public.

Building a Group Behavior Covenant

The covenant is written to serve the youth on the event. It should be written to ensure that the everyone present respects each person and that each person respects the group experience. It is signed as a symbol of mutual trust. A group-created covenant helps youth in your group learn to take responsibility for their actions. The group takes the responsibility of being faithful to the covenant, rather than placing the burden of rule enforcement on the adult leaders.

A clearly worded statement needs to be drafted, discussed, and perhaps amended by those attending until it can be adopted by the youth and adults on the trip. The statement is then presented to each participant, who agrees to it as a prerequisite for going on the trip. Have the covenant printed at the top of a sheet of paper that is passed around for each person to sign before each travel event. Or the covenant can be printed on the registration form, with a blank for the participant's signature.

Sample Covenant

Event: _____

Date: _____

In signing this covenant, I agree to live by the following guidelines listed below during the event in order to fulfill the purpose and vision of our youth ministry:

(*List your youth ministry vision statement here.*)

I shall:

1. Respect the health of my own body by refraining from the use of tobacco and drugs of any kind, except those prescribed by a physician.
2. Respect the physical and emotional well-being of other youth and adults by "doing unto them as I would have them do unto me"

(Luke 6:31, adapted). This includes respecting the need for sleep, refraining from harmful practical jokes, and so forth.

3. Respect the property of the places we will be visiting.
4. Be responsible for my own behavior and participate fully in all scheduled activities of this event and abide by group decisions made during the event.

(You can include a question that asks each youth to indicate what exactly he or she is willing to do during the event that will contribute to the viability of the covenant.)

Signature: _____

A Sample Retreat Schedule

There is no limit to what a schedule can look like, but following is a fairly typical arrangement.

Friday night

8:00—Arrive and unpack gear.

9:00—Gather; discuss rules; clarify agenda; answer questions.

9:30—First session: theme development; establish prayer partners; sing.

10:30—Whole-group active movement/recreation, movie option, snacks.

12:00—Evening wind-down via share groups and devotions.

12:30—Lights out.

Saturday

8:45—Breakfast (Remember, sleeping in can be a gift.)

9:30—Gather; review agenda; answer questions.

10:00—Second session: sing.

10:15—Second session: presentation/theme development.

11:30—Break for lunch.

1:00—Organize free-time options, such as soccer game, pool, volley-ball, hiking, and preparation for evening talent show.

5:00—Supper.

7:00—Gather; review agenda; answer questions; chat.

7:30—Third session: sing.

7:45—Third session: presentation/theme development.

8:30—Special evening activity: talent show.

10:00—Snacks and break.

10:30—Game: high energy.

12:00—Devotions and cool down.

Sunday

Breakfast, not too early.

9:30—Gather; review schedules for packing up, cleaning up, loading vehicles, and other issues; sing.

10:00—Fourth session: sing.

10:15—Fourth session: presentation/theme development.

10:45—Closing worship event.

11:30—Pack; load; head home.

Traveling With Youth

Assuming the event goals are clear and attainable, you've now got to put it on the road. Taking any kind of trip for any distance with any number of people requires planning and preparation. Whether moving four people across town or moving busloads across the country, planning will make things smoother.

Attendance

Is this a senior high trip only, a junior high trip only, or for everyone? Estimate realistically, by name if possible, the youth who might attend. Add in the number of adults required (one adult for five to six youth is ideal) to make the event safe. When those numbers are tallied, is the trip still feasible cost-wise? This is important because none of the other areas below can be dealt with until some sense of participation, including a good guess of how many females and males will attend, is firmly stated.

Transportation

- **Cars**

Traveling in a car is usually the cheapest way to go, and it is certainly the easiest to plan. Cars get excellent gas mileage, and because most people have one, you don't have to rent.

- **Vans**

If your numbers are too large to fit into a car or several cars, then it is time to move up to the next size: a van. A van presents some different issues. Where will you put the luggage? Do you need a trailer? Do you have a hitch? Is a driver available who can safely maneuver a van with a trailer? If your church doesn't have access to a van, explore renting one. Are there people in your congregation with a van who would be willing to go along?

- **Bus**

  If you have a large group, a bus may be the safest and most manageable way to travel. When renting a bus, find out the total costs involved (price per mile, driver expenses, and so forth). The initial price of a bus may sound high, but when divided by the number of people traveling, it may be within your budget.

Lodging

Anytime a trip continues into the night, you need to give some thought to how sleeping arrangements will be handled. Options include:

- Tents/camping.
- Hotels (Give attention to tips and taxes, which sometimes are as high as eighteen percent. Room quotes seldom include this amount, and it adds up quickly.)
- Churches.
- Colleges (In summer, dorms lack linens, sometimes even light bulbs.)
- Inexpensive motels (Why pay for extras such as pools and hot tubs, especially if arrival is after those kinds of amenities are closed?)

Meals

Here are some options for dealing with meals while traveling:

- Expect all the youth to bring extra money for their own meals; whenever a food stop is made, they are responsible for their own meals. They should know in advance exactly how many meals and which type of restaurants will be frequented.
- Collect all the money ahead of time. At each food stop, hand them an appropriate amount for that meal.
- Buy groceries and prepare meals for the group at appropriate meal stops.
- There are times when all three methods should be blended for an event.

When you're buying groceries, be aware of special dietary needs and limitations. Some youth may be diabetics or vegetarians; others may have allergies or be on a diet; all have preferences.

Travel Costs

Reviewing the following areas should put you on track for moving your group safely to and from home. Consider the following:

- Materials: You need all the little extras: maps, guidebooks, propane tanks for the stove, paper plates, and utensils. Can any be borrowed, or should all of it be purchased?
- Adults: If an adult is willing to go on a trip with the youth, his or her expenses should be provided, if not completely, to some significant degree.
- Entrance fees: Parks, campgrounds, tickets to attractions—all need to be rolled into the bottom-line cost. Figure the whole package out ahead of time so the participants are not caught off guard during the trip.
- Trip insurance: This may be available through your local church or through the annual conference. It's not expensive; it just has to be taken care of ahead of time.
- Contingency fund: Carry enough cash to get you out of an average jam. Other more serious emergencies can be put on various credit cards and settled later.
- Fine print in contracts and forms: Make sure every question has been asked and all special situations have a ready response.

The cost of the trip can be divided evenly among the youth, backed by a trip budget, raised totally by the youth through activities, or some combination of the three. However it's done, think through the whole plan carefully before you go too far in planning or signing a contract.

Combination Trips

Some groups have had positive travel experiences by combining purposes. These types of trips could include the following:

• Recreation/Touring/Study

The group travels to a particular location, taking advantage of sightseeing and recreational opportunities, as well as concentrating on an area of study—for example, a ski trip with Bible study and sharing at night. Or the group might travel to a location related to the area of study—for example, touring a prison and observing juvenile court while studying the Christian's response to prison reform and the death penalty. Study during a campout could focus on God's creation and on our responsibility to take care of it.

- **Work/Recreation**

    The group members travel to donate their labor to a work project, such as poverty home repair. They also take advantage of recreational opportunities in the area.

- **Mystery Trips**

    Youth sign up for this type of trip without knowing the destination. Clues may be given, but only adult leaders and parents know where the group is going. The advantage of this kind of trip is the interest and excitement it can generate. The disadvantage is that youth are not involved in the planning.

Retreat Checklist

Supplies

- ❑ Extra Bibles
- ❑ Nametags
- ❑ Room assignments
- ❑ Rules or covenant
- ❑ Retreat schedule and evaluation handouts
- ❑ Lesson plans/handouts/paper and pencils
- ❑ Cameras/film/batteries
- ❑ Videos/monitor/extra connection cables
- ❑ Song sheets/songbooks, musical instruments
- ❑ Audiovisual equipment
- ❑ Equipment for games and activities
- ❑ Worship candles, Communion elements, and so forth
- ❑ Petty cash

Food

- ❑ Snacks
- ❑ Meals (if not provided)
- ❑ Beverages
- ❑ Special dietary considerations

Travel

- ❑ Maps and clear, correct directions
- ❑ Full tank of gas
- ❑ Jumper cables
- ❑ Insurance card, registration

❑ Telephone number and name of manager on duty at site posted at the church and with a parent

Emergencies

❑ First-aid kit

❑ Name, address, and directions to nearest hospital while at the retreat site

❑ Completed permission slips and medical release for every person. Make sure your medical release form complies with the laws of your state and the policies of your congregation. You may want to talk with someone from a local hospital to find out what is required in your state. Your church insurance agent and church legal counsel are other possible resource people.

❑ Name and phone number of parent who will notify other parents in case of emergency or change of plans

For More Help

Go For It: 25 Faith-Building Adventures for Groups, by Walt Marcum. Published by Abingdon Press. Available through Cokesbury (800-672-1789).

Retreats from the Edge: Youth Events to Build a Christian Community (Essentials for Christian Youth), by Paul Harcey and Edge Ministries. Published by Abingdon Press. Available through Cokesbury (800-672-1789).

Great Retreats for Youth Groups: 12 Complete Faith-Building Weekends, edited by Chris Cannon. Published by Youth Specialties.

Chapter

Resources, Methods, and Strategies

What Are Resources?

God puts opportunity before us consistently, day in and day out. Too often we fail to recognize it for what it is. The key is to see things for what God may be trying to say to us. In considering resources, everything and anything is subject to God's purposes.

Resources Are Media

- Books of programs, games, and great ideas; public libraries and other church libraries.
- Videos, cassette tapes, compact discs.
- Computers, the Internet, CD-ROMs, faxes.
- Movies, television, plays, drama, and poetry.

Resources Are People

- Preachers and teachers.
- Youth workers and youth.
- Writers of poetry and journals.
- Tellers of experiences, thoughts, and reflections.
- Professionals and experts in the community and congregation.

Resources Are Natural

- Trees, wind, thunder, lightning, songbirds.
- Rising and setting of the sun and the moon; the twinkling stars as we ponder God's universe.
- Tactile feelings of liquids, heat, breezes, pain, body movement, ice, and food.

Resources are everywhere we look and everywhere we touch, feel, and think. With an abundance of potential resources around us, ask,

"What can they do for us? How do they help us in our youth ministry? What does God want us to learn? What resources has God provided?"

The best resources are those which:

- Engage youth physically and actively in learning.
- Invite youth to participate by making a contribution and a difference. Too often youth feel they make the effort to attend, but their presence doesn't seem to make a difference, and no one cares.
- Invite a personal response from the participants: thinking, feeling, imagining, questioning, mind-stretching, spiritual questing, decision-making, growing in faith, and taking action.
- Enable youth to make a difference, sharing a bit of who they are and what they know for the good of the whole community.

Using Resources

What can resources provide? Think of resources as you would an encyclopedia. To make an encyclopedia work, you must already have an idea of what you want to find—a topic, theme, or subject. No one walks into class and begins teaching by reading from a book labeled "Volume A to D." That's not how an encyclopedia is supposed to work. We have to have some sense of where we want to go. Then we have to open its volumes and look for things that equip, share, and bring light to what conforms to our focus.

Anyone can use resources effectively; age is no limitation. All that is required is patience and research. Don't overlook other people as a place to get great ideas. Try your hand at identifying a need that fits within the goals of the ministry; name a theme; and begin! In no time you can develop a knack for pulling various ideas and activities into an engaging time.

In considering any resource, follow these steps:

- Approach resources with some notion of a goal—a theme, an idea, or a topic that you know is germane and of interest to them and that serves your overall vision.
- Determine the big idea in the materials or suggested activity. Can you state it in your own words? Put another way, "What do you want to get across? Where do you want to go?"
- How can the core idea be best communicated with our particular teens? Think about the youth individually. Then think about which method(s) will best communicate the core idea to them.

- Plan, but stay flexible. Have a plan for opening, continuing, and ending. Aim for widespread participation. Adapt resources to fit the amount of time available. Don't try to cram in too much. If the discussion takes an unplanned turn, let it go that way as long as it seems helpful and is not too far from the goal.

Selecting Resources

In selecting resource materials that will be effective for your youth group, ask the following questions:

- Is the resource truly suited to your youth? Is it too simple, or is it over their heads? Is it designed for the age level using it? Does it duplicate content or methods recently used? Is it relevant to the concerns of your youth? Does its focus fit your vision of youth ministry?
- Will the resource truly help you achieve your goal? Will it really help move you in the general direction of your overall vision? Does it do what you want to do?
- How much adaptation or reworking will the resource require? Program materials often have to be adapted to fit specific needs and situations. Adaptation is commendable because it shows that the youth using the resource are trying to make it truly their own. But large-scale reworking can be time-consuming. If this route is necessary, be sure the project is worth it. If not, look for another resource better suited to your theme.
- Will your budget stand the expense? Obviously, some resources cost more than others, so weigh them carefully.
- If the resources are not published by The United Methodist Church, ask these questions: Is the resource biblically, theologically, and educationally sound? Does it reflect a theology consistent with that of The United Methodist Church? Ask your pastor or Christian educator to help you evaluate the resource you are considering.
- One of the strengths in using United Methodist resources is that they are designed and developed under the mandate of The United Methodist Church to be biblically, theologically, and educationally sound. They are by no means the only sound resources available. Other denominations produce excellent resources as well. However, resources produced by The United Methodist Church are designed specifically for use by United Methodists

and can help us learn about ourselves as United Methodist Christians.

- If your group is not clear on the basics of our denomination, what would be required to change that? Using materials that are consistent with United Methodist beliefs requires some basic understanding of what those beliefs are. What procedure should be followed to set up some meetings where these topics are discussed? Is there someone who would be willing and able to teach this material creatively?
- Consider creating your own resources. This takes time and a degree of self-motivation, but it can be rewarding. Test your ideas with others; consult specialists in youth ministry around your area, especially youth, who can serve as listeners.

Resource People

Pastor

Ask your pastor to help the youth ministry become more involved in the congregation by encouraging youth participation in worship and in the congregation's administrative groups. Your pastor's theological training is a rich source of knowledge for biblical study, and it provides a perspective for discussing current events. Your pastor can be helpful in counseling youth and in helping them develop their own skills as peer pastors or counselors. Get to know your pastor. Reach out to include him or her as a valued member of the congregation's youth ministries.

Parents

Parents can be more than chauffeurs and cooks. These are people who have a particular interest in the health of the youth ministry and who have experience and skills to share. Get to know the parents of youth in your group, and use their areas of expertise in your programming. While some parents may not be especially interested or supportive, others will connect with your group. How can you get to know these folks?

- Include a rotating parent or guardian representative on your planning team.
- Meet in youth member homes occasionally, perhaps once a month.
- Have a "parent night" once a quarter when youth bring their parent(s) or guardian(s). Activities can include cookouts, recreation, discussion of parent-teen communication, movie or television evaluation, and worship.

- Have a parents' meeting every six months to share your plans for the ensuing six months, with sign-up sheets available for activities that need parental assistance.
- Invite a resource person from the community to speak on an issue of concern to parents of youth.
- Invite a small group of parents to establish a support group for parents of youth that might meet monthly or bimonthly at a time that coincides with a youth meeting.
- Meet with parents or guardians for short-term studies to deal with concerns, such as how to improve communication or how to prepare their youth for the future. Youth may support this by helping with promotion and publicity and by suggesting topics of study that the youth would like parents to consider. This is one way the youth can include ministry to parents as an ongoing program.

Other Members of the Congregation

Your church and community have many adults with diversified skills. A little creative thinking can produce ways to use these people for retreats, meetings, or a short series of classes. Consider the following as a way to begin thinking about this.

- A homemaker can speak on issues of time management.
- Young couples can be resource people for dating and marriage issues.
- A contractor can serve as advisor for a work camp.
- A school counselor can participate in a discussion on occupational futures.
- A judge or attorney can talk on the subject of the law and ethical decision-making.
- Someone from the church finance committee can speak on the matter of money management.
- A physician can help youth understand sexually transmitted diseases and other issues related to sexuality.

Methods for Discovering Concerns

Leading learning experiences that appeal to a variety of learning styles takes planning. Always determine your purpose or goal first. Then choose the method that will best enable you to fulfill your purpose. Many different methods can be used. This list is a sampling of some you may want to consider.

- Incomplete sentences. The beginning of a sentence is given for a person to complete; for example, "I think prayer is like . . ."
- Word associations. One word is given; people are asked to give other words that come to mind and discuss.
- Artistic expressions. List, draw, or paint ideas, concepts, problems, concerns, feelings, or dreams. Feelings and ideas are expressed in original symbols or words.
- Writings. Write your own creeds, prayers, or poetry.
- Spiritual autobiography. Write or draw a spiritual autobiography. Persons write their own faith story with words or symbols or a graph line showing the ups and downs.
- Interviews. Find out a person's or a group's opinion on a given subject. This can be done live or tape-recorded.
- Inventories, checklists, or questionnaires. People are invited to respond to a list of questions or statements compiled before the activity.
- Personal experiences. People are invited to share their own experiences concerning a particular subject.
- Brainstorming. Ideas are expressed verbally with no judgment made about any idea. A time limit is set at the beginning. All ideas are recorded. This enables new ideas to emerge from the group. Evaluation occurs after the time limit has expired.
- Quiz games. Concepts concerning the subject are presented in a game show format.
- Graffiti sheets. These are similar to incomplete sentences. Words or symbols are printed at the top of a large blank sheet of paper or freestanding box. People are invited to respond anywhere on the paper or box.
- Continuum or agree/disagree statements. Designate one end of the room as "agree" and the other end as "disagree." The leader reads aloud controversial statements. People place themselves in proximity to one of the walls to indicate their response to the statements.
- Symbols. Thoughts and feelings are expressed by creating an image with modeling clay, pipe cleaners, wire, and so forth.
- Banners, posters, or buttons. Using paper, fabric, markers, paint, or yarn, illustrate one or more simple ideas.
- Montages. Create a picture by combining several examples from one medium (printed words, photos, magazine ads, and so forth).

- Collages. Create a picture using two or more media (photos, printed matter, paints, fabric, three-dimensional objects, and so forth).

Methods to Stimulate Discussion

These methods can be used to spark discussions. Use them either as the opening activity or as an exploring activity to help persons deal more in depth with the subject that has been presented.

- Artistic expressions. List, draw, paint, or write in response to a discussion question.
- Open-ended problem situations. Group members are given a situation and must decide what happens next.
- Roleplay. Assume the role of a character in a given situation and act out that character in either a predetermined or a spontaneous way.
- Cartoons and ads. Analyze the messages. Write new messages for the pictures, creating new pictures for the messages. Create an ad or cartoon to express the idea being studied.
- Reaction to art forms, symbols, magazine and newspaper articles, stories, poetry, or music. Use them to stimulate the group's thinking.
- Interpretive dance, mime. Perform movements to words or music to express a particular subject.
- Demonstrations. Enable the group to observe how something functions that is related to the subject.
- Acrostics. This is an arrangement of words in which certain letters spell another word.
- Case studies. Express opinions in response to questions about what the characters said or did in the example being studied.
- Questions and answers. Ask questions that are thought-provoking to stimulate thinking.

Discussion Groupings

- One-to-one. Pairs share personal experiences or interview each other.
- Groups of three: participating and observing. One gives his or her opinion; one asks questions or listens; and the third observes the other two. Group members switch roles until each has experienced each role.

- Quiet meeting. The group sits in silence until one person feels moved to speak.
- Circular response. Going around the circle, each person in the group is invited to speak. Persons may pass. Everyone is given a chance to speak once before anyone can speak twice.
- Debate. Present arguments for and against a subject.
- Fishbowl. The group sits in a large circle with several people sitting in an inner circle. People in the outer circle observe, while people in the inner circle speak. Outer circle participants are encouraged to speak by placing an empty chair in the inner circle where they can sit or by tapping an inner circle person on the shoulder to exchange places with the outer circle person.
- Small-group discussion. This is for groups of three to six people; each group discusses for a set period of time, then reports back to the total group.

Top Ten Ways to Lead a Discussion

- Do your homework. Try to be as informed as your participants.
- Get people to sit in a circle; don't let anyone sit outside the circle.
- Good discussion won't happen if the group is too large. Break it down so there are no more than eight to ten maximum in each group.
- Fashion questions so individuals can share their knowledge before you start telling them what you know.
- Learn to offer feedback in ways that clarify and emphasize a person's main point.
- You don't have to agree with everything, but you do have to be cordial and understanding.
- Don't ask questions that can be answered with a yes or a no. If you get that response, always follow up by asking, "Why?"
- Don't let anyone dominate the conversation.
- Don't single anyone out or put anyone on the spot, especially those who are quieter.
- Summarize the main thoughts or any decisions the group makes before departing.

Presenting Information

You can present content in many ways other than by giving a lecture. Use the methods listed in this section to help your group interact with the subject being studied.

- Simulation games. A life situation is simulated in a game format.
- Field trips. The group visits a particular location to gather information, to investigate a problem, or to be confronted with a real-life situation.
- Learning centers. Places where youth interact with resources are selected to help them gain better understanding of the subject. This may include listening, viewing, reading, or other activities.
- Timelines. Chronological listings of past and/or projected events related to the subject are shared.
- Charts and maps. Reproductions of information related to the subject are presented in a concise form. This shows how different aspects of the subject are related to each other.
- Quotations, stories, or case studies. Make selections to present information and/or insight about the subject in a thought-provoking way.
- Puppets. Use them to help hold a group's attention while presenting information.
- Interpretative dance, mime.
- Skits and dramatic readings. Brief dramatic presentations are either written by the group or are acted out from a script provided.
- Roleplaying.
- Then and now. A historical person in costume "visits" the group. Or the group reads about a historical situation and then rewrites it in a modern setting, perhaps acting it out.
- Shadow playing. This involves performing a pantomime or story play behind a white sheet, with the playing area backlighted so that the audience sees the action as shadows projected on the sheet.
- Audiovisuals. Show video clips, movies, or pre-taped youth presenting an idea.
- Visuals (art, overheads, bulletin boards, and so forth).
- Recordings (compact disks or cassette tapes).
- Directed listening, reading, or viewing. Listen, read, or view, according to guidelines suggested by the leader.
- Research and share. Have a person find particular information about a subject and then share it with the group.

- Soapbox. Express a problem, peeve, or point of view for a limited amount of time (perhaps two minutes).
- Panel or panel forum. Two or more people with special knowledge of a subject hold a conversation guided by a moderator in front of the group. It becomes a panel forum when the audience directs questions to the panel.
- Symposium. Several speakers deliver short addresses on the subject or related subjects.
- Resource person. A person with extensive knowledge of a subject shares with the group. He or she may or may not try to persuade the group to his or her point of view.
- Lecture or illustrated lecture. A carefully prepared oral presentation is made by a qualified person. The presentation may be illustrated with visuals.

For More Help

For information about United Methodist curriculum resources and program materials, call the toll-free Curricu-U-Phone help line (800-251-8591) or e-mail curricuphone@umpublishing.org.

Cokesbury is the official distributor of resources for The United Methodist Church. Visit your local Cokesbury store or the Cokesbury website (**www.cokesbury.com**). The toll-free Cokesbury order number is 800-672-1789.

Many annual conferences have a media library from which you can check out videos, tapes, and other resources. Check with your conference council on ministries office to see if a media library is available in your area.

Let's Talk About It: How to Lead Discussions With Youth (SkillAbilities for Youth Ministry), by David Miles Burkett. Published by Abingdon Press. Available through Cokesbury (800-672-1789).

Chapter

14

Expanding the Vision

OtheR Youth—SeRving ORganizations

Partnering with other youth-serving organizations is a way that churches can extend their ministry. Four youth agencies that are found in many local congregations are Camp Fire Boys and Girls, Boy Scouts of America, Girl Scouts of the USA, and 4-H. Each of these agencies offers a unique opportunity to minister to young people. These organizations are particularly appropriate if you are attempting to develop community-based outreach ministries for children and youth.

Boy Scouts of America

Target audience: boys, ages 7-20, and girls in Venturing, ages 14-20.

Primary emphasis: development of character, citizenship, and self-reliance through small-group activity.

Program structure: small-group structure, youth interaction with adult role models.

Special features: extensive drug prevention and youth protection programs, high adventure bases.

Girl Scouts of the USA

Target audience: girls ages 5-17 or kindergarten through twelfth grade.

Primary emphasis: leadership development, service to others, skill development, and career exploration.

Program structure: small-group structure with girl/adult partnership.

Special features: contemporary issues series, leadership institutes, math and science partnerships, national and international events.

Camp Fire Boys and Girls

Target audience: boys and girls from birth through age 21.

Primary emphasis: stresses the development of the whole child through goal setting and problem solving.

Program structure: small-group structure; youth interaction with adult role modeling.

Special features: programs for short-term subjects in addition to club programs.

4-H

Target audience: boys and girls from kindergarten through twelfth grade.

Primary emphasis: acquiring knowledge and skills for life; becoming productive in society.

Program structure: structure varies depending on type of club.

Special features: variety of programs available, including national events.

God and Country Program

The God and Country Program is the religious recognition program designed for use by the Boy Scouts of America, Camp Fire Boys and Girls, and the Girl Scouts of the USA. However, any youth who is a member of a Sunday school class, vacation Bible school, confirmation class, or other church group is welcome to use the God and Country Program, whether or not he or she belongs to a civic youth organization. To earn this award, youth need to complete the requirements in the student workbook under the supervision of a counselor (either the pastor or someone appointed by the pastor).

God and Country Programs are available for the following groups:

God and Me, grades 1–3; God and Family, grades 4–5; God and Church, grades 6–8; and God and Life, grades 9–12.

Youth Covenant Discipleship Groups

A Youth Covenant Discipleship Group is a group of approximately eight to ten youth who, together with an adult mentor, develop a covenant that states the ways in which they would like to be better disciples. The group meets weekly for about an hour to report to one another on how well they have kept the covenant during the week.

Covenant Discipleship Groups are based on the class meetings origi-
nated by John Wesley as a method of accountability and spiritual
growth.

Each group's covenant has statements in four areas: acts of compassion, acts of justice, acts of worship, and acts of devotion. While each
group develops its own covenant, the following sample covenant is typical for many groups.

- We will read the Bible daily.
- We will avoid talking about other people.
- We will care for our bodies.
- We will pray each day.
- We will attend worship weekly.
- We will attend our Covenant Discipleship Group weekly.

Chrysalis

Chrysalis is a three-day spiritual retreat modeled after the Walk to
Emmaus. Chrysalis is open to sophomores, juniors, and seniors in high
school. It is a weekend filled with surprises and heightened understanding of God's grace. Teens who attend Chrysalis can find answers to
questions they have about Christian faith, prayer, Bible study, being a
friend, sharing their faith with others, and being a spiritual leader in
their local church. Attendance at a Chrysalis retreat requires finding a
sponsor who has attended an Emmaus or Chrysalis retreat.

Disciple Bible Study for Youth

DISCIPLE is a powerful model of Bible study that is focused not only
on facts, but also on learning what the Bible has to say about living the
life of a follower of Christ. DISCIPLE uses many different teaching techniques that appeal to the diversity of learning styles among youth and
adults. DISCIPLE lasts nine months. It is not focused on reading every
verse of the Bible, but is instead centered on reading major portions
and understanding broad themes.

The youth edition of DISCIPLE features a small group (no more than
twelve) and an adult facilitator. The group makes a covenant to read
about an hour per day and to attend weekly sessions that last ninety
minutes to two hours. Each week the participants make notes on their
reading and share insights gained. The group then watches a twenty-
minute video of a biblical scholar who speaks on the theme for the

week. The key portion of the weekly session is called "Marks of Discipleship." The group members discuss how they can apply their reading and particular disciplines to their faith life. Because of the time and commitment required, the group grows together spiritually, builds a trust level, and becomes a supportive community.

Youth Ministry Is Family Ministry

Every family is different. No measuring stick exists by which to judge families normal or abnormal. Families of youth are found in many different configurations. Some of these include:

- Single parents with children.
- Grandparents raising grandchildren.
- Foster families.
- Two parents with children.
- Blended families with children from previous marriages.
- Older siblings raising younger siblings.

The church cannot replace the family unit. However, youth ministry can strengthen and support families by being "pro family" in mission, vision, and aim. This includes:

- Communicating constantly and effectively. Communication is vital. Letting parents know what you're planning is much more effective and appreciated than depending on youth to relay information. Also share with parents/guardians the goals and vision of the youth ministry. Ask them to offer ideas of how the youth ministries can be supportive and helpful to the family.
- Remaining mindful of the tremendous scheduling pressures of most families.
- Making it easier for youth to participate in family time by scheduling fewer but higher quality events and activities.
- Providing resources and opportunities for families to be together.
- Building rapport and relationship with parents/guardians.

Being in Ministry With Families

Provide Assistance

Many parents/guardians feel unskilled and unable to do their job. The church can assist them by:

- Offering parenting classes or support groups.

- Purchasing books for personal and group study.
- Planning parent-youth discussions.
- Offering workshops on family dynamics, human sexuality, family spiritual growth, and playing together as a family.

Form Cluster Groups

Create family clusters, groups of families that gather from time to time to have conversation about what it means to be a family. Try to include in those clusters at least one family in which a parent is gifted in relating to youth. This kind of relationship will encourage growth in individual families and among all the participants.

Provide Spiritual Opportunities

Youth ministry as family ministry is faith-oriented, focused on the process of assisting families in their spiritual growth. Encourage families to worship together, pray together, and think together. Encourage families to grow together in their relationship to God. ·

Involve Parents in Youth Ministry

Some youth are comfortable with their parents being in a leadership situation with their youth group, while others are far less so. It is always important to ask a youth how he or she feels before inviting a parent to come along on a retreat or to accept a leadership or advisory role. Involving parents and other family members says that those people are important and that they are part of the team. Youth ministry is a team effort, a family process. Gone are the days of keeping parents and family out of youth ministry.

Remain Flexible

Family structures are continually changing. Ministry to families with teenagers is a process that requires constant listening. Specific family needs must be discovered and rediscovered through a regular system of assessment and goal setting. Adopt an attitude of flexibility and willingness to change or to modify programming.

Youth Ministry Is School Ministry

The local school system is another potential partner for ministry. Work with school administrators and teachers to promote healthy lifestyles. Attempt to plan events and activities that will complement rather than compete with school schedules. You could plan a dance or a party to begin after a game. You could serve a meal before a play or concert. Try not to plan an important retreat or event during playoffs or exams.

While most schools do not allow adults to roam the halls, there are ways that volunteer and professional youth workers can be involved at school. Some schools will allow adults to visit students for lunch. Some schools use adult volunteers in classrooms. It is imperative that adults who want to go on school campuses receive permission from the school administration.

Other ways to support youth include playing games and attending concerts and plays. Sitting with parents at these events is a great way to build relationships with them.

Youth Support Groups

Many communities have a variety of support groups available for youth and others who have specialized needs. Usually these groups are led by those with training in a particular area. Some congregations form support groups for particular groups, providing both the facilities and leadership; and some congregations form partnerships with other community organizations to provide facilities for support groups. Putting a youth in contact with an appropriate support group is often an important ministry. Find out where the agencies are, what services are offered, what the cost (if any) is, and what the referral process is. Provide help for youth and their families by making contacts and referrals.

In many communities you will find support groups for the following:
- Survivors of violence, incest, abuse, and trauma.
- Eating disorders.
- Dealing with grief and loss.
- Youth whose parents are separating, divorcing, and re-marrying.
- Single-parent families and blended families.
- Teenage parents.
- Addicts and alcoholics.
- Teens who cannot communicate with their parents.
- Parents who cannot deal with their children constructively or positively.

Twelve Step Groups

In many communities Twelve Step groups are developing as needs are identified. These are groups for youth and adults who want to deal with addictions and behaviors in a spiritually centered environment. They are based on the Alcoholics Anonymous model of admitting powerlessness over behaviors and situations; giving them up; trusting God to help overcome them; and relying on others for insight, leadership, and encouragement.

The value of these and other groups is that they are designed to empower persons to deal with their own realities. They provide opportunities to develop coping skills and to learn life skills for living with, overcoming, and even removing, attitudes, behavior, and conditions that inhibit personal growth. Support groups restore self-confidence and self-esteem. They provide relationships and nurture.

Parachurch Ministries

The word *parachurch* is based on the Greek prefix *para,* which means "alongside of" or "beside." In our context, youth ministries that have evolved independently from any denominational ties are commonly referred to as "parachurch." Ministries such as Fellowship of Christian Athletes, Youth for Christ, Young Life, Meet at the Pole, and InterVarsity Christian Fellowship are specific examples of parachurch. These ministries are not stand-alone ministries or substitutes for congregational youth ministry. If we truly stand beside one another, how can we magnify cooperation and collaboration?

- Begin by clarifying your vision for ministry. How might parachurch ministries and local church youth ministry move toward a common vision? A shared vision is an invitation to work together. If spreading the gospel to youth is a primary goal, the parachurch group and local church youth ministry teams are colleagues, not competitors.

- Discern which teens the various groups are trying to reach. Some groups target any youth not involved with a church. Others try to reach youth in crisis by visiting jails. Some single out youth who have common affiliations, such as sports or interests in a specific kind of Bible study or faith sharing. Churches tend to relate first to youth of families who are members of the congregation. It will serve your youth leadership team well to know who is and who isn't being addressed and cared for.

- Once visions and audiences are clear, respond creatively to the parachurch groups who work alongside and with church youth ministry. What ways can you be in ministry together? Look for points of commonality. Try to reach agreement on strategies for ministry. Foster a spirit of cooperation instead of opposition. Don't become adversarial; be an ally whenever possible.

Guarantor Ministries

Young people need to relate to mature Christian adults who model committed relationships that are not cast aside because of conflict or disappointment. Many of today's young people have not experienced this kind of enduring love. A nurturing relationship with a mentor can demonstrate the power of a committed, enduring relationship grounded in Christ and in Christian principles.

The concept of a guarantor or a mentor has been used for many centuries by craftspeople. A person wanting to learn proficiency in a particular trade would make a covenant with a master in that field. By trading labor for the privilege of learning the intricacies of his or her chosen profession, the apprentice and the guarantor achieved mutual economic and knowledge exchange. The apprentice advanced in status as he or she acquired the fine arts of his or her particular craft through hands-on experience. This was a common practice before the industrial revolution and the advent of our present school system.

A reliable and caring guarantor relationship may help a youth gain a healthy sense of self-esteem, and that in turn helps the youth cope better with life's stresses. A guarantor in a young person's life is an adult who will listen and who can be trusted with confidential information. This adult is also available to answer important questions concerning the youth's doubts, hopes, fears, and faith issues. Youth learn how to deal with adults other than parents through relationships with guarantors. In this relationship, youth have the peer-free opportunity to ask questions and to share doubts about faith and spirituality. This relationship aids youth in developing and strengthening their faith, as well as in helping them connect the faith of the church community with the reality of life.

Following are some suggestions for developing a guarantor ministry.

- Identify adults who are willing to give the time and effort necessary to establish a nurturing relationship.
- Invite adults to be prayer partners with youth.
- Target at-risk youth (from both the church and the community) for long-term support, guidance, and acceptance.
- High school juniors and seniors may benefit from either a long-term or a short-term relationship with a guarantor who helps them struggle with changes such as graduating from high school, joining the military, entering college, or joining the work force.
- Guarantors are not limited to adult/youth partnerships. Older youth may be paired with children in specific settings, such as midweek tutoring during the school year or a summer experience at vacation Bible school.
- Take care in advising guarantors how and where to meet. Guarantors should abide by all church policies and procedures for working with children and youth. Fast-food establishments are often good places to meet, since there are others present, and the familiarity of the setting is more relaxed.
- Guarantors should possess high moral and ethical standards for themselves and for the youth they are mentoring.
- The church should provide an advisor for the guarantors who can help them understand and fulfill their responsibilities.

For More Help

For information about civic youth-serving organizations:

Boy Scouts of America
1325 West Walnut Hill Lane
P.O. Box 152079
Irving, TX 75015-2079
Website: **www.bsa.scouting.org**

Camp Fire Boys and Girls
Dept. W, P.O. Box 804452
Kansas City, MO 64180-4422
Website: **www.campfire.org**

4-H
Check with your County Extension Service.
Website: **www.4h-usa.org**

Girl Scouts of the USA
420 Fifth Ave.
New York, NY 10018-2798
Website: **www.gsusa.org**

Office of Civic Youth-Serving Agencies/Scouting
P.O. Box 859
Nashville, TN 37202-0859
Phone 615-340-7129 or 800-509-4563

**To order God and Country resources or
for more information, contact:**

P.R.A.Y.
8520 Mackenzie Rd.
St. Louis, MO 63123-3413
Phone 800-933-7729
Website: **www.praypub.org**

For information on Youth Covenant Discipleship Groups:
Together In Love: Covenant Discipleship For Youth, by David
Sutherland. Published by Discipleship Resources. Available through
Cokesbury (800-672-1789) or Discipleship Resources (800-685-4370);
website: **www.discipleshipresources.org.**

For information on Chrysalis:
Additional information on Chrysalis is available at the Upper Room
website: **www.upperroom.org.**

For information on DISCIPLE:
Information on Youth DISCIPLE is available through Cokesbury (800-
672-1789).

For information on guarantor ministries:
Friends in Faith: Mentoring Youth in the Church, by Barbara Bruce
and Chuck Kishpaugh. Published by Discipleship Resources. Available
through Cokesbury (800-672-1789) or Discipleship Resources (800-685-
4370). Website: **www.discipleshipresources.org.**

Chapter

15

Leadership
Issues

Checklist for Effective Group Leadership

The designated leader, youth or adult, has a lot of power and responsibility in the beginning stages of a group. The group members look for and expect the designated leader's guidance in matters of what will be done and who will do it in the group session. It will take time for the group members to develop the confidence and security to assume leadership roles themselves.

Basic skills for effective group leadership include an ability to:
- Listen to others.
- Summarize where the group is.
- Ask questions in specific ways to guide the group in a needed direction.
- Cope with conflict when it arises and deal with a hidden conflict when the group is ready to be challenged.
- Be patient when the group needs to struggle with an issue.
- Distinguish between your own personal needs and the group's needs.
- Share leadership functions within the group without being threatened that you will lose control of the group.
- Be comfortable with group silence.
- Keep the group focused on issues rather than on personalities.
- Help the group do problem solving and evaluation.

An effective leader will be the kind of person who:
- Is accepting God's grace each day and is responding by placing his or her will and love in God as revealed in Jesus the Christ.

- Demonstrates faithfulness to the vision of the youth ministry.
- Knows how to express warmth and to be a friend.
- Thinks and says "we" and "our" more than "I" and "my."
- Knows his or her own abilities and uses them wisely.
- Is ready to learn and ready to admit what he or she does not know.
- Knows how to delegate responsibility.
- Is dependable in following through on what he or she agrees to do.
- Says thank you to youth and adults for their contributions—both as leaders and as followers.
- Strives to understand others.
- Listens to others, tries to appreciate their points of view, and accepts those who disagree with him or her.
- Seeks to learn more about his or her particular job responsibilities.
- Knows how to be supportive of others.
- Encourages others to develop their leadership skills.
- Is not satisfied with "the way we've always done it" and can think through new possibilities.
- Dares to dream and works to realize these dreams.
- Is accepting, loving, responsible, dependable, and committed to God in Christ.

Adult Leader Attributes

Effective youth ministry does not exist without adult leaders. In fact, probably the most critical factor in an effective youth ministry is the ongoing presence of adults who are caring, competent, and committed in their work with young people.

The basic quality needed to be an effective adult youth leader is appreciation for youth and for what they can do. Other skills can be learned. An effective adult leader is someone who:

- Cares about young people and their faith journeys.
- Knows how to work with people to help them learn leadership skills.
- Is willing to take risks both in relationships and in program.
- Is open to other persons and ideas.
- Has a commitment to honesty in speech and in relationships.
- Knows when to be firm and when to be flexible.
- Is dependable, loving, realistic, and utterly human.

- Believes youth ministry is important enough to give it his or her best efforts.
- Has a sense of humor.
- Is willing to listen more and talk less.
- Is free of concern for stereotyped marks of success (large numbers in attendance, personal recognition, and so forth).
- Reveres the opportunities of any given moment.
- Finds joy and excitement in sharing experiences with youth.

An effective adult leader with youth is not:
- A top sergeant.
- A hovering, smothering guardian.
- Someone who says, "I'll be there, but don't expect me to do much."
- A person in need of a following.
- A person searching for a lost adolescence.
- Someone looking for spiritual merit badges.
- A procrastinator.

The question is not, "What may I do for these young people?" but "How may I be present with these young people in an authentic, vulnerable, compassionate, and committed way?"

Skills for Leadership

You need certain skills to help a group grow as a loving, caring fellowship of young Christian disciples. Very few people have all the needed skills. This is another important reason to have a team of adult leaders so the adults can complement one another. These skills can be divided into three basic categories: relational, organizational, and spiritual guidance.

Relational Skills

Relational skills refer to the person-to-person ways we relate to individuals and to a group as a whole. These skills are the heart of youth ministry. If youth feel an adult is interested in them, identifies with their concerns, and is open to their thoughts, feelings, and ideas, they are likely to participate in a mutual learning and caring fellowship. On the other hand, if young people feel put down by an uncaring and inflexible adult, they will look for any excuse to avoid participation. Relational skills include:

- Listening actively with not only ears, but also with eyes, emotions, wisdom, and heart.
- Responding with concern, encouragement, affirmation, and non-verbal gestures.
- Enabling others to identify and to use their gifts and abilities.
- Communicating trust.
- Being approachable to listen to deep hopes and concerns.
- Being sensitive to individuals and situations.

Organizational Skills

Organizational skills can make the difference between an average experience and one that is exceptional. Organizational skills include:

- Planning ahead.
- Showing courtesy in returning phone calls and responding to questions.
- Monitoring to ensure that some youth do not dominate while others are excluded.
- Providing resources for purposeful ministry.
- Selecting and scheduling to create sustainable youth ministry. It's human nature "to bite off more than we can chew."

Unnecessary problems can be alleviated by the following:

- Creating opportunities for training youth in leadership skills.
- Providing appropriate advice as it helps youth grow in Christian discipleship and form Christian values.
- Seeing the whole picture to ensure a well-rounded program of service, worship, fellowship, outreach, and study.

Spiritual Guidance Skills

We cannot effectively guide others where we have not been ourselves. The best way to develop spiritual guidance skills is to be actively practicing spiritual disciplines in your own life. Traditional spiritual disciplines include:

- Individual and corporate prayer.
- Participating in Holy Communion on a regular basis.
- Conversation with other Christians for accountability in discipleship and for discernment of God's calling.
- Participating in worship.
- Regular reading and meditating on the Scripture.
- Fasting.

Matters of Discipline

Maintaining discipline (in the usual sense of this word) is not a primary goal of United Methodist youth ministry. Rather, achieving behavior that allows the group to function responsibly, productively, and enjoyably is seen as the essential task. Discipline is not the sole responsibility of a single adult. Most volunteers serve in the role of advisors, not police officers.

The most desirable discipline comes from within an individual, not superimposed from the outside. To promote inner discipline that will bring about desirable, cooperative behavior, consider the following:

- Have the group draw up a list of guidelines for the well-being of the ministry, understanding from the outset that this will be a statement based on mutual respect and the common good of all.
- Use the guidelines as a ministry covenant.
- Review the guidelines from time to time to remind participants of the agreements and to provide opportunity for updating, if necessary. Throughout the whole process, adults should serve as advisors and participants, sharing their concerns and identifying areas that are non-negotiable because of the nature of the ministry.
- Discuss the need for inner discipline as discipleship—the root word is the same—as necessary for growth as individuals and as groups.
- Carefully explain to the youth involved why the guidelines exist and why they must be adhered to. Simply imposing rules flies in the face of shared responsibility. No one likes to be told what he or she can and can't do without logical and rational reasoning and an opportunity for input.
- Act in a caring manner in all instances, particularly when a guideline has been violated and some action is required.
- Allow for some mistakes to be made, and be willing to practice forgiveness in the deepest sense. These will be opportunities for you to model God's grace.

When There Is a Paid Youth Worker

If a paid staff person is responsible for working with youth, the role of the adult volunteer remains as critical as ever. It's important to agree on responsibilities, however, so there is a minimum of confusion. Here are some clues that might help.

Meet Regularly

Communication between the staff person and the supporting leaders of the youth ministries is essential. Leaders will probably need to meet at least monthly to coordinate tasks, calendar, and concerns. Additional meetings might include an annual spiritual life retreat, a recreation and leisure escape, or regular Bible study.

Know the Roles and the Rules

Exactly which tasks and responsibilities belong to the staff person? Normally, a youth director or pastor has responsibility for the youth program and must have adult leaders to support the various ministries within that big picture. The staff person also serves as a primary resource person, able to recommend many kinds of assistance to the supporting adult and youth leaders.

Creating a Team of Adult Colleagues

An effective youth ministry system cannot exist without committed adult leaders. Finding adults who are caring and committed both to Christ and to youth is the most critical factor in an effective, long-term youth ministry. Finding, training, and nurturing these volunteers is a perpetual task and deserves much prayer and thought. The following steps can assist you in the process.

Know What The Specific Task Is

People respond best when they have plenty of specific details. Some specific questions are:

- Exactly what am I being asked to do?
- How much time will it take? per week? per year?
- How long will my responsibility last?
- Who will be working with me? How much experience do they have?
- What resource materials are available to help me?
- How is this ministry financed? What will I be expected to contribute?
- What training is available? How can you help me acquire the training that I need?
- Will this ministry automatically put me on other church committees or councils?

- What other ongoing meetings of youth (such as leadership groups or teams) will I be expected to attend in addition the task I am being asked to do?

Focus on the Gifts of the Individual

Rather than making a general plea, look for and identify specific people who have the gifts or skills needed. After identifying a person who has the temperament, the ability, and the time to do the ministry needed, approach him or her. Point out the gifts that individual has and other aspects of why he or she has been identified. Give the person time to think about the situation, and then follow up a day or two later.

People enjoy and appreciate using their gifts and skills. When they recognize that someone is asking them to do a specific job, they think to themselves, "Someone who knows exactly what is needed has thought through this and believes I can do the job!"

Identifying Specific Tasks

Youth ministry is often more manageable when it is divided into different tasks, with individuals (youth or adults) taking responsibility for a specific task. One task might be as a greeter, standing at a main door for half an hour welcoming teens as they enter. That's all this person does. Greeters wouldn't be expected to lead a discussion or Bible study, to say prayers, or to do any of the things for which they might feel unqualified and thus would choose not to get involved.

Other examples are:

Announcements

Perhaps someone has a certain flair for helping youth do this with humor and creativity. For example, someone could videotape youth making announcements and show it later for different gatherings throughout the week or month.

Parking Lot Attendants

Because many youth ministry opportunities take place at night, parents derive a great deal of comfort knowing there is an adult in the parking lot. This person makes sure the youth are safe as they move from the cars to the meeting site and back again.

Bible Study Leaders

This person might be good at Bible interpretation, talking, leading, and teaching. He or she does not have to be adept at or interested in games, counseling, cooking chili for thirty people, or the latest football scores, just leading Bible study.

Retreat Organizer

This is someone who handles arrangements for travel, overnight stops, retreat centers, campsites, and so forth. This person handles details, organizing and monitoring the overwhelming details in these undertakings. This person may be uninterested in leading the program at the retreat, but can wonderfully handle the technicalities of organizing the food, kitchen, meals, and other organizational tasks.

Special Project Coordinator

A person might be willing to organize a once-a-year event such as a fundraising event. This task would include working with a youth leadership team, planning, promotion, organization, food, and invitations.

Prayer and Share Leader

This person might have a gift not only for praying but also for teaching prayer and involving others in helpful and meaningful ways.

As you can see, there is a limitless number of roles or task possibilities. Each time there is a new and specific task, find a way to name it. Once a task is named, identify a person to claim it, one who will then work to get others involved. Inch by inch each program becomes an event staffed with leaders willing to give their time in specific capacities with agreed and set limits.

Recruiting Leaders

To truly set someone free for ministry in the name of Jesus Christ, we must see people first and their problems second. That certainly holds true as you choose your youth leaders. The following suggestions should help:

- See with God's eyes. Observe and name what a person enjoys and does well. See people as God does, looking for the gifts they have. Sometimes people do not recognize their talents as gifts at all. The obvious may be hidden from them. For these people, your naming their gift becomes a powerful motivator.

- Offer this person an opportunity to use his or her gifts with others to the glory of God. Give credibility and encouragement to the person for the things he or she does well.
- Allow this person creative latitude to use her or his gifts. Creatively find ways for this person to gain confidence in leading.

Involving Youth in Identifying Adult Leaders

Another form of authentic youth ministry is involving youth in thinking through, selecting, and inviting potential adult leaders.

- Begin your recruiting process by asking the youth to list desirable qualities for adult leaders.
- After a thorough discussion of this list, ask the group to identify various people within the congregation who have these qualities.
- Be careful to guide this process and prevent it from degenerating into a gossip session about various people's faults and shortcomings.
- Select who will contact the individual(s) selected and how it will be done. Should they use a letter, a home visit, a special youth meeting, or should it be done over lunch? Will the invitation come from the youth, from youth and adults, or from adults representing youth?

Training Volunteer Leaders

1. One of your primary sources of training for adult youth leader is the youth themselves! As you open yourself to these children of God, you may be amazed at how much you will learn from them.

2. A second source is other adults who are experienced as adult youth leaders. They can be helpful in the following areas:
   - Introduction to program resources: finding them, adapting them, using them.
   - Relational skills development.
   - Organizational skills development.
   - Spiritual guidance skills development.
   - Planning.

3. Contact your district and conference coordinators of youth ministries for a schedule of upcoming training events. If you have

special training needs, let them know. These people may be able to plan a training event to include your needs.

4. District and conference coordinators of youth ministry are sometimes available for on-site training in churches. If they cannot come, they can probably recommend other people qualified to do such training.

5. The General Board of Discipleship sponsors a national training event for adult workers with youth every other year. Contact your conference youth coordinator for details.

6. Don't overlook training opportunities right in your own community. Hospitals and other social service agencies frequently conduct workshops and seminars that pertain to youth ministry. Call these agencies and get on their mailing lists.

7. Take advantage of events offered by other churches in your area. Join with them to bring in professionals that your church might not be able to afford by itself. Capitalize on the event later by creating an interdenominational support group of employed and volunteer youth leaders in your community that meet on a regular basis.

8. When training new adult youth leaders, consider the following:
   - Invite these people to sit in on several youth sessions in order to begin to know the youth and to become familiar with the format.
   - Provide resource materials (to be used in training as well as with youth) well in advance so that new leaders can become familiar with the resources and can refer to them easily in the training event itself.
   - Explain the steps you use in planning.
   - Explain the work of the planning groups in the leadership model you are using and the adult worker's relationship to these groups.
   - Provide time for the new leaders to ask questions and to react to experiences.
   - Let the new leaders know you are available to support them as they learn this new job.

Diversity in the Adult Leadership Team

The greater the variety of adult youth leadership, the more likely it is that a particular young person will find at least one adult he or she can relate to as a friend, role model, and spiritual guide. When selecting adults for youth leadership try to seek balance in the following areas:

Age

Young adults provide energy and enthusiasm and are close to the youth in age. Single people may provide examples of commitment to career and to God. Middle-aged adults who are not parents of the youth involved provide parenting role models. Older adults provide wisdom, perspective, and time to interact with young people.

Family Configuration

Whether with children or without children, couples with solid relationships can model for the youth the healthy "give and take" that marriage can be.

Parents and Guardians

Parents can be one of your best resources, whether they become regular youth group leaders or not. When considering parents, also consider the desires of their youth. Some youth enjoy having their parents involved; others do not.

Skills and Abilities

Look for individuals that bring different traits to the team:
- Humor and entertainment.
- Clear theology and steadfast faith.
- Games and athletics.
- Crafts and artistic ability.
- Writing and publishing.
- Nursing and first aid.
- Counseling and family therapy.
- Music.

Legal Responsibilities

When adult leaders of youth spend time with young people in any setting, we promise to protect them from physical and emotional harm. Even if the church has not explicitly made such a promise, the legal system of our country considers it implicit and binding. Your church may have policies and procedures in place to increase safety and reduce risk. All workers with youth should be aware of these policies and should abide by them. If a teen comes to you and informs you that he or she is being sexually abused, or if you have evidence to lead you to believe that abuse is occurring, you have an immediate legal obligation to report it. Your church policies might guide you through the reporting process.

If your church does not have policies and procedures developed, these are some steps to start the process.

Develop a Written Conduct Policy

Any institution that involves itself with children and youth must have a policy in place that addresses sexual misconduct, abuse, and accidents. A clear written policy addresses:

- Definitions of abuse and areas of concern.
- Response procedures and reporting practices.

The policy should be reviewed:

- By a local attorney for compliance with state laws.
- By the church insurance company.
- By the agency that investigates reports of child abuse and misconduct.

Screen Workers

Set up procedures to screen people who have or seek to have contact with children or youth. A questionnaire should be used to acquire information that will help confirm:

- Positive identity, including a request for a photograph.
- Where they previously attended church.
- What roles they filled at the previous church.
- What non-church work was done.
- What qualifies them for working with youth now.
- If they had any training in dealing with matters of sexual misconduct.
- If they have been convicted of or pleaded guilty to a crime.
- If they have a current driver's license and, if so, what is the driver's license number.
- Personal references complete with addresses and phone numbers.

Also create a consent form to authorize a criminal records check with the police. It's important to have a complete form for every person. These forms should be kept together in a safe, confidential file.

Train Workers

Provide training for all workers with youth and children to make them familiar with the policies and procedures that have been developed.

Three basic guidelines in working with youth are:

- The two-adult rule. At no time is any adult to be alone with teens.
- In any overnight situation, adults must not sleep in the same bed with a youth. Exceptions are only for a father and son or a mother and daughter. In hotels, where rooms are shared, rollaway beds are recommended.
- Never be the first to hug or the last to let go.

Written Policies

Ensure that you have procedures and processes for:

- Medical release forms and when to use them.
- Permission forms—always use them.
- Vehicle policy—who can drive and what training they should have.
- Worker screening procedures.
- Supervision and training procedures.
- Reporting outlines.
- Handling the media procedures.

The big picture of these liabilities should give us pause. While daunting to consider, this can become a catalyst to grow closer, more aware of, and more sensitive to the genuine issues teens face each day. This is a process through which a team can become more effective and more confident in its ministry to and with youth and with one another.

Give prayerful consideration to these and other issues of legal responsibility. Use this topic as a reason to bring in specialists who can guide and inform on these topics. When the initial labor is done, and the procedures are in place and working, your overall youth ministry will have a new luster and depth that will serve youth and families in your community well.

For More Help

Safe Sanctuaries: Reducing the Risk of Child Abuse in the Church, by Joy Thornburg Melton. Published by Discipleship Resources. Available through Cokesbury (800-672-1789) or Discipleship Resources (800-685-4370); website: **www.discipleshipresources.org.**

SkillAbilities for Youth Ministry Series, published by Abingdon Press. These twelve, small, easy-to-digest books are packed with ideas, skills, tools, and inspiration. They are an excellent resource for training adults who work with youth. Available through Cokesbury (800-672-1789).

Forum of Adults in Youth Ministry (FAYM)

This national organization has a membership made up of those persons interested in or working with youth ministry. For more information check their website at **www.umc.org/nymo/faym.html.**

Chapter

16

We Are United Methodist

A Connected Church

People move for many reasons: college, a job, or some kind of opportunity. Moving is uncomfortable because familiarity is lost. Regardless of where one moves, he or she probably will always be able to find a familiar United Methodist community of faith nearby. These connected churches rely on the same basic language, format, and operating procedures. In the chaos of moving and traveling, there can be a great deal of comfort and security in being a part of the connection that we call The United Methodist Church.

Another strength of "the connection" is that it encourages people to work together and to share resources. Sharing and striving together is much more productive than working individually and is a great model of Christian stewardship. Ministries sponsored by the congregations, districts, annual conferences, jurisdictions, central conferences, and general church unite our denomination to be an effective witness of God's gifts.

Organization of The United Methodist Church

Local Churches

The first and most basic unit of organization is the local church, referred to as the charge. Sometimes more than one church is served by the same pastor, creating a multi-point charge. The local church is where we gather for worship, outreach, and nurture. Administration in the local church is by laity and clergy working together. Laity and clergy cooperatively provide leadership for all forms of ministry in the local church.

Each year the leadership of the charge meets in what is called charge conference. This is where church officers are elected.

Districts

Districts provide churches in a given region opportunities to work together more closely and to support one another. Each district has a unique name, different from the other districts in the same conference. Oversight of the district is provided by the district superintendent, a clergy person appointed to the position. Many districts have a district coordinator of youth who helps coordinate youth ministry at the district level.

Annual Conferences

Each local church is located within a district, and each district is located within an annual conference. The term *annual conference* refers to both the geographical boundaries of the conference and to the yearly meeting of the members of the annual conference. The membership of the annual conference includes all the clergy members of the conference and at least an equal number of lay members. Each local charge has at least one lay member of the annual conference who is elected by the local church charge conference.

Oversight and spiritual leadership for the annual conference is the responsibility of the presiding bishop. The bishop, working with the district superintendents (called the cabinet), appoints clergy to serve in local congregations and other places of ministry.

The annual conference can offer opportunities for mission and service that are beyond the abilities of a local congregation. Many annual conferences sponsor camps, volunteers-in-mission trips, and training opportunities.

Most annual conferences have a coordinator of youth ministry. Some annual conferences have a full- or part-time staff person who also works with youth ministry at the annual conference level. These people work with and for youth to effectively handle programs and events for the youth in their conference area.

Jurisdictions

Each jurisdiction is composed of various annual conferences in a specific geographical area. The United Methodist churches of the United States are in five jurisdictions: Western, North Central, South Central, Southeastern, and Northeastern.

Every four years each jurisdiction holds a jurisdictional conference. The members of the jurisdictional conference are elected by the annual conferences. There are an equal number of lay and clergy members. One of the primary functions of the jurisdictional conference is to elect bishops.

Central Conferences

In areas outside the United States annual conferences are organized into central conferences. These conferences meet every four years. There are seven central conferences: Africa, Central and Southern Europe, Federal Republic of Germany and West Berlin, German Democratic Republic, Northern Europe, Philippines, and West Africa.

General Conference

The General Conference meets every four years and is composed of equal numbers of laity and clergy elected by the annual conferences. General Conference is the only body that can speak officially for The United Methodist Church. Some of the responsibilities of General Conference include defining the conditions, privileges and duties of church membership; defining the powers and duties of clergy; providing a hymnal and ritual for the Church; and enacting legislation that will become part of *The Book of Discipline* (the book of law for The United Methodist Church).

Youth Ministry Beyond the Local Church

The United Methodist Church is a connectional church. Every church is a member of a district, and several districts make up an annual conference. Several annual conferences combine to form a jurisdiction. Youth ministry is organized along these same lines.

District Youth Ministry

Many districts have a district council on youth ministries composed of youth representatives from the churches of the district. District youth councils provide programs and organization to support youth ministry in all the churches of the district. They can hold regular meetings, and they can sponsor occasional worship rallies or mission opportunities/ training for youth adult leadership. The district coordinator of youth, typically appointed by the district superintendent or elected by a district program council, serves as one of the adult advisors.

Annual Conference Youth Ministry

Youth from all churches in the conference have an opportunity to serve on and to be served by a conference youth ministry structure. Youth and adults are selected or elected, usually through district channels, to work with the conference coordinator of youth ministries. Together these groups constitute what is called in most conferences the conference council on youth ministries. Their purpose is to develop ministries that enrich youth ministry throughout the conference.

The conference council on youth ministries meets as needed to outline policy, to set budget, and to plan special emphases and projects. These might include training youth and adult leaders; organizing institutes, assemblies, and camps; enabling youth representation and participation in the ministry of the annual conference; and suggesting resources to use in district and local church programming. The conference council should, in cooperation with the district councils on youth ministry, help youth in every church carry on their ministry more effectively and live more abundantly as Christian disciples.

The conference youth council is also responsible for promoting the Youth Service Fund and for administering its portion of the Youth Service Fund.

Jurisdiction Youth Ministry

In each jurisdiction there is a jurisdictional youth ministry organization that meets in a convocation at least every other year. This organization includes four voting representatives from each annual conference in the jurisdiction. This group is responsible for electing three youth members and one adult member to serve on the National Youth Ministry Organization Steering Committee.

In some jurisdictions the jurisdictional youth ministry organization also initiates jurisdictional camps, conferences, training, and other events that serve to strengthen youth ministry.

The National Youth Ministry Organization (NYMO)

The National Youth Ministry Organization (NYMO) is the vehicle through which youth can express themselves in a united way to the general church. Its purpose is not to direct the youth ministry program on all levels (local, district, conference, and jurisdiction). Rather, NYMO listens to youth on all levels because it is composed of youth from all levels. Then NYMO communicates what it hears to the general church. NYMO has three basic units: Convocation, Legislative Assembly, and Steering Committee.

The purpose of NYMO is to:

- Be an advocate for youth and for the concerns of youth.
- Empower youth as full participants in the life and mission of the church.
- Be a forum for the expression of youth needs and concerns.
- Provide a means of outreach through the Youth Service Fund.

The NYMO Convocation meets biennially and is responsible for providing leadership training, opportunities for spiritual growth, and strengthening connectional youth ministry. Any United Methodist youth or adult worker in youth ministry may participate in the Convocation.

At the NYMO Legislative Assembly, annual conference delegations of three voting delegates—two youth and one adult—come together to accomplish several things:

- Raise major concerns of the youth the annual conference delegations represent, and bring those to the attention of the general or national church.
- Empower youth throughout the church, through the support of communication with annual conference and jurisdictional youth ministry structures.
- Determine the policy and criteria for selection of projects and distribution of the national portion of the Youth Service Fund.
- Select monetary goals for the Youth Service Fund.
- Provide an opportunity for youth and adults from throughout the church to share and to grow in Christian commitment for discipleship.

The NYMO Steering Committee includes four elected representatives from each jurisdiction (three youth and one adult). This group carries on the work of NYMO between convocations. The Steering Committee administers the national portion of the Youth Service Fund; selects projects to receive funding from the national portion; plans and implements the convocations; convenes the NYMO Legislative Assembly; and communicates the actions of the assembly to the appropriate places.

For More Help

NYMO staff offices are in Nashville, Tennessee. Questions about NYMO, the Youth Service Fund, the convocation's legislative assembly, and NYMO priorities may be directed to the NYMO Office, P.O. Box 840, Nashville, TN 37202-0840 (telephone, 615-340-7184; e-mail, NYMO@aol.com).

Questions about the organization and structure of The United Methodist Church and its ministries with youth may be directed to Office of Youth Ministries, General Board of Discipleship, P.O. Box 840, Nashville, TN 37202. E-mail at umyouth@gbod.org, or during business hours call toll-free 877-899-2780.

For current press releases and other information on The United Methodist Church, visit the website at **www.umc.org**.

For general questions about The United Methodist Church, call InfoServ toll free, 800-251-8140.

Appendix
www.gbod.org/youth

The General Board of Discipleship website provides up-to-date information on a wide variety of topics related to youth ministry. Bookmark this site and visit it frequently. On this site you will find:

- **Updated information about topics covered in the UMY Handbook (www.gbod.org/youth/UMY_appendix.html).**

- **Discussion board with others interested in youth issues.**

- **Events for youth and youth leaders.**

- **Mission opportunities.**

- **Articles on cutting-edge issues in youth ministry.**

- **Links to other youth-related sites.**

- **Resource listings.**